MALAWI

A. Hülsbömer
P. Belker

BRADT PUBLICATIONS, UK
HUNTER PUBLISHING, USA

Contents

Part I: Encounters in Malawi - Past and Present   7
Missionaries in Malawi   7
'Flue' and 'Burley' in Malawi   16

Part II: The Country Malawi   19
Historical Aspects   19
Economic Aspects   27
Geographical Aspects   31
President Banda   52

Part III: Travel Guide   59
General Information in Brief   59
Transport   63
Equipment   69
Money Matters   72
Health   74
Accommodation   80
Malawi Through The Photographer's Eye   81
Culinary Delights   82

Part IV: The Cities   87
Karonga   87
The Official Capital: Lilongwe   87
The Unofficial Capital: Blantyre   93
The Former Capital: Zomba   98
Fort Johnston/Mangochi   100
Livingstonia   102

Part V: National Parks and Natural Wonders   105
Cape Maclear   105
Nyika National Park   108
Kasungu, Lengwe and Liwonde National Parks   111
Game Reserves   131
Hiking in the Mulanje Mountains   131
Likoma Island   134

Glossary   **137**
Index   **139**

First published in English in 1991 by Bradt Publications, 41 Nortoft Rd, Chalfont St. Peter, Bucks, SL9 OLA, England from the German original by Conrad Stein Verlag, Kiel.
Distributed in the USA by Hunter Publishing Inc.

Copyright © 1991 Conrad Stein Verlag

All rights reserved. No part of this publication may be reproduced, stored in a retrieval system, or transmitted in any form or by any means, electronic, mechanical, photocopying or otherwise without the written permission of the publisher.

ISBN 0-946983-52-6

Translated from the German by Bettina Oehrling
Photographs by Frank Hülsbömer
Maps by Heinz Grün

THE AUTHORS

André Hülsbömer, born in 1966, studies political economy and history in Trier, Germany. He also studied one semester in Dublin. He works as a free-lance journalist in Trier; his travel accounts on east Asia and Africa were published in various German newspapers. In 1988/89 he carried out a research project about African trade unions together with Peter. The reports (part 1) and the regional studies (part 2) of this book are written by him.

Peter Belker, born in 1965, studies business management and marketing in Trier. He also studied for one semester in Dublin. In 1988/89 he carried out a research project about African trade unions together with André. Peter Belker wrote 'Travel Guide' (part 3), 'The Cities' (part 4) and 'National Parks and Natural Wonders' (part 5).

Frank Hülsbömer, born in 1968, is a photographer with his own studio in Münster, Germany. He specializes in advertising photography and portraits. Frank took all photographs in this book, including the cover photo and wrote the section 'Malawi Through the Photographer's Eye'.

PART I

Encounters in Malawi - Past and Present

MISSIONARIES IN MALAWI

A Mission's Centennial

For Londoners, April 18, 1874 was a special day: the day on which the beloved hero of the newspaper front pages is laid to eternal rest in Westminster Abbey. His name was David Livingstone, Scottish explorer and missionary in Southern Africa. His body was buried without the heart. Eleven months ago loyal servants had cut it out and buried it underneath a tree in Tanganyika where Livingstone's last journey ended. He was found dead on May 1, 1873; he died during his morning prayers. From now on the former cotton spinner would rest next to royalty. This honour was never before bestowed upon an explorer, except Christopher Columbus. Among the guests attending the memorial service was a certain Dr Stuart from Lovedale, South Africa, a missionary of the Free Church of Scotland. He was deeply impressed by the event and decided to put his idea of founding a mission in Central Africa into practice. After the funeral he left for Scotland where he introduced his plan to the chapter of the Presbyterian Free Church. The Scottish Church had been thinking of founding missions in Africa for some time. As missionary work in Southern Africa had been successful, it was time to concentrate on new tasks. Within a very short time a commission was called to organize the journey. In honour of the deceased the new mission was called Livingstonia Mission.

One year later, in May 1875, a group of young men were ready to embark. Captain E.D. Young of the Royal Marines, familiar with the tropics, led the mission. The area around Lake Nyasa (today's Lake Malawi) was their destination. Further members of the expedition were: Dr Robert Laws (physician), a serious pragmatic man in his prime who was second in command, John McFayden (engineer), Allan Simpson (engineer), Alex Riddel (farmer), George Johnston (carpenter), William Baker (sailor) and finally Henry Henderson, the man who had to choose the location for the mission station. He had worked in virgin Australia and was therefore considered an experienced explorer. Stuart did not take part in the first expedition, but planned to follow with a successive group a year later.

In Six Months Around the World

The professions of the group members showed that religion was not the driving force behind the undertaking. No, the scientific goal of exploration came first, the religious mission came second. The first stage of the journey was to Lovedale mission station in South Africa where the Scots chartered a schooner. They sailed northwards to the mouth of the Zambezi river on the Indian Ocean. Part of the equipment was a small dismantled steamer called the Ilala, which was put together as soon as they had reached the Zambezi. From now on they continued the trip on the Ilala. When the group was struggling against the current of the Zambezi they could at least resort to Livingstone's diaries for guidance. He had studied the course of the Zambezi and its tributaries and thereby discovered the Victoria Falls, the magnificent waterfall which he had named after the Queen. About 180 miles upstream they branched off on the Shire River, which they knew was fed by Lake Nyasa. The journey caused no problems until the men reached the Murchinson rapids on the Shire. The Ilala could not pass the turbulent waters. Yet the Scots, who knew of this particular difficulty from Livingstone's writings, were prepared. The Ilala was hauled up on land and dismantled. 8,000 porters carried the pieces on their heads over the mountains to the lake where the little ship was put together again. At the end of this extravagant and bold undertaking sailor Baker stated that there was not one bit missing. After a six-months journey, on October 12, 1875, the expedition came to a peninsula on Lake Nyasa which Livingstone had named Cape Maclear after his friend, an astronomer. One of the engineers describes the longed-for arrival at the lake in his diary:

"The engines were switched off and the steam was released. We assembled on deck to celebrate a short service. Dr Laws said, 'let's sing together Psalm number 100' and we sang with all our might:

All people that on earth do dwell
Sing to the Lord with cheerful voice
Him serve with mirth, Him praise for tell,
Come for ye before Him and rejoice (...)

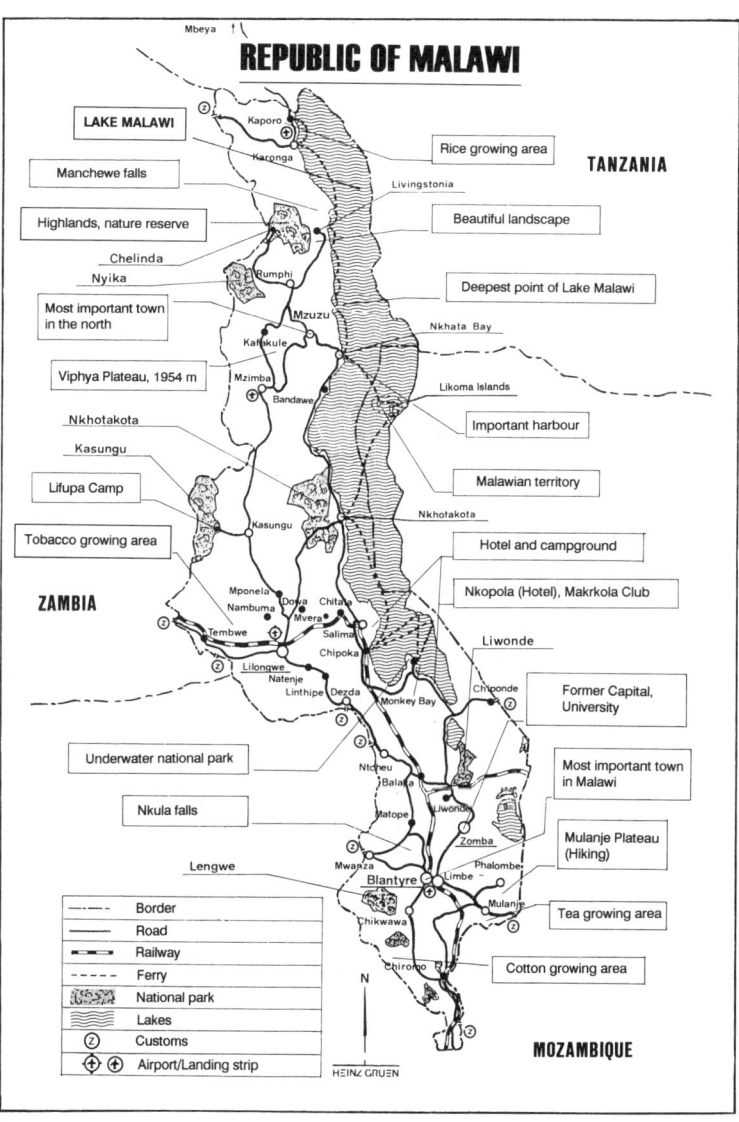

For why? The Lord our God is good
His mercy is forever sure
His truth at all times firmly stood
And shall from age to age endure.

It was a touching moment."

The expedition pitched camp in a sheltered bay at the west side of the peninsula. The nearby fishing village provided them with food. Thus Cape Maclear became the first Livingstonia mission site.

The pioneer Henderson left the crew of the Ilala to construct the mission house and moved southwards, looking for a suitable place for the first outstation. He climbed Zomba plateau and explored the entire Shire Highlands until he finally rediscovered a region which Livingstone had mentioned in his diary. The area between the Ndirande and Soche mountains was rich in wood, fresh water, and fertile soil, the people were friendly and the Shire waterway was not far. Henderson named that piece of land Blantyre, after Livingstone's birthplace.

Seven Poor Years

In 1876 the second expedition, led by Dr Stuart, followed. Four black Evangelists from South Africa, Ng'unana, Nthintli, Wanchope and Koyi took part in it together with Dr William Black (physician), Robert S. Ross (engineer), John Gunn (agronomist) and A.C. Miller (weaver). Yet the second expedition was ill-fated. No sooner had the men settled at Cape Maclear than the climate caused two deaths: Dr Black and Shadrach Ng'unana died of fever. Dr Laws, who had become leader of the mission, was desperate. Ng'unana had been a friend to him over many years. Laws wrote to Scotland: "Maybe we put too much hope in him and his work. God may have chosen those men who seem to be less apt to complete his work."

Koyi was one of the less apt. He said about himself that he was only half-talented, but he devoted himself to missionary work with all his heart. Thanks to him it was possible to communicate with chief Ngoni who lived with his people in the northern area of the lake. Koyi spoke the language of the natives and was capable of passing on to them the Word of God. In 1877 however, missionary work was far from being successful.

In the Middle of Slave Traders and Tribal Feuds

It soon became obvious that Henderson had chosen a bad location for the mission. Except for the fishermen in Chembe the Cape Maclear area was very underpopulated and tropical diseases were a permanent threat to the missionaries' lives. Thus plans were made to move the mission, but only after three more people died were the Livingstonia headquarters moved to Bandwe on the west coast of the lake. Back home in Scotland the organizers almost lost faith in the project. Looking back over the past five years a shocking conclusion was made: 5 deaths, £20,000 of expenses and tropical adversities on the one hand and one convert in Blantyre and a deserted mission site at Cape Maclear on the other. That is not exactly what the fathers of the project had had in mind. In spite of all these hardships the missionaries continued their work. Faith in God and the mission to show the natives of central Africa the way to the kingdom of heaven kept them going. The Holy Bible clearly stated what their mission was: go out and tell it from the mountain. A series of failures showed Bandawe not to be a good choice either. The countryside was hard to explore, the climate nearly as intolerable as at Cape Maclear. On top of this Bandawe belonged to the territory of the Tonga, a tribe which was permanently at war with its northern neighbour, the Ngoni. The mission site was in the heart of the war zone. Exceeding all bounds were the slave dealers, who raided the area around Bandawe at regular intervals to recruit more slaves.

Broken Spell

Koyi, the half-talented, advanced towards the north where he was unexpectedly successful. In doing so he was the one who decided the mission's future. In 1882 Koyi established an outstation in Njuyu, opened a school, and provided the population with medical care. When he died, four years later, he had already laid the foundations for missionary work in Nyasaland. The Ngoni turned out to be friendly, open-minded and curious. Consistent work bore its fruits. At regular intervals waves of Ngoni, willing to convert to Christianity, flocked to the mission. One day, in 1889, 309 adults were baptized. Good news was also recorded from Blantyre. The Blantyre mission supplement *Life and Work* claimed the same year: "This year we sold 181 hymn-books, 24 testaments written in Yao and one Bible written in English. There is further demand for Bibles and testaments, but we ran out of stock." The population was more than grateful for schooling facilities and hospitals. In 1890 a total of 5,000 pupils attended classes in 26 schools of the Free Church of

Scotland. And beer-brewing women promised God to produce the devilish stuff only in small quantities from then on. For the first time since the Livingstonia mission settled on the shores of Lake Nyasa, their work was crowned with success.

Expansion Underway

In the end, Dr Laws decided to move the headquarters of the mission for a second time, due to the area's barely endurable climate and tribal feuds. This time the location was to be final, it would be the umbilical cord of the mission. On September 21, 1884, at the beginning of the hot dry season, Dr Laws, his latest colleague Dr Elmslie, and Uriah Chirwa, one of the first Tonga converted to Christianity, set out to search for a new location. On the Ilala they travelled northwards following the west coast of the lake, anchoring off shore from the small fishing village of Chilumba where they took drinking water and food aboard. From the lake, towering rocky walls were to be seen, several ravines with dense vegetation and finally, at the northern end, a long mountain ridge. Dr Elmslie suggested climbing the ridge. There was no path to follow, just waist-high grass, thick underbrush which was an ideal hiding place for all kinds of beasts. No white person had ever set foot on that patch of earth before. In the evening of October 12, after two days of climbing, the three men reached a plateau. Two days of suffocating heat lay behind them, in the mornings there was not even a trace of dew on the grass. On top of the mountain the two Scotsmen found an almost familiar landscape. Sweet-smelling meadows of flowers, rambling hills. What they could not see nor suspect from the shore was that the trees stopped abruptly below the plateau, allowing a breath-taking view over the immense Lake Nyasa. Visibility to the north reached as far as the frontier of German East Africa (today's Tanzania). To the east, beyond the lake, it reached to the green and brown highland area of Portuguese East Africa, now Mozambique.

Why did they choose that place? What made them climb that particular rocky part of the shore? In his diaries Dr Laws simply stated, "We were directed there". The same evening all three of them had the feeling that their search had come to an end. The next morning they found their restless anticipation of joy confirmed. The view from the plateau was magnificent. Upon first examination the plateau was found to be ideal level ground. And mosquitoes, carriers of the insidious malaria parasite, were rare at such windy heights. There was drinking water in abundance, the villagers of the small Ngoni settlement Khondowe adopted a wait-and-see attitude, remaining friendly. Dr Laws decided to stay at the place which would be Livingstonia, the new and final headquarters of the mission. Both Scots returned to Bandawe in order to organize the move while Chirwa remained to prepare the construction of the first huts. Bamboo frames were erected and plastered with loam. The missionaries' first residences were built.

Missionary Work - Construction Work
The following 20 years were characterized by an inconceivable progress in both the construction of the towns Blantyre and Khondowe and the Livingstonia mission. Hundreds of natives, working on the building site, established contact with the missionaries. They did not work for charity alone, but for British cloth. In 1891 the roofing ceremony of the first solid Christian church between the Zambezi river and the Nile, called St Michael's and All Angels Cathedral, was celebrated in Blantyre. In 1896 lamps illuminated the streets at night. A post office was built and next to it the Mini-Clock-Tower, a copy of London's Big Ben. Dr Laws' residence, Stone House, was completed in 1903.

From between 1908 and 1911 the David Gordon Memorial Hospital was built, as well as storehouses, schools, shops, houses, work-shops, a cathedral and a great number of other buildings. In 1905 Livingstonia was provided with piped hot and cold water, a year later a small hydroelectric power station was built, which is still working today.

In 1902 construction of a 12-mile long mountain road was begun, leading from the shore of the lake to the mission site. Today the same red dirt road winds through the bushes to a height of 3,000 feet. In 1896, after long and drawn-out preparations, a theological faculty was founded in Livingstonia. In 1914 Hezekiah, Tweya, Jonathan Chirwa and Yesayah Zerenji Mwasi were the first ministers of the Presbyterian Church to receive holy orders. They were the first African priests ordained at Livingstonia mission. After 40 years the circle of missionary work was completed. Since then Livingstonia mission has built African roots and now grows independently.

Education and Black Emancipation
With the outbreak of World War I in Europe in 1914 the mission from Scotland finally met with success. The new century brought 'Christian

awakening' to Nyasaland. In 1914, 40,000 baptized Christians and a network of 860 schools, scattered over the whole country, belonged to the mission. In 1914 the first step towards an independent African church was made. The first Malawian priest from Livingstonia symbolized the first farewell to the white missionaries.

World War I meant a severe setback for all missions in Africa. Numerous members of the missions joined the army voluntarily, others were enrolled for compulsory military service. Schools had to reduce their staff. Theological, technical and medical faculties in Livingstonia and the whole of Nyasaland were closed. After the end of the war there was a deficit in white personnel, trained according to European standards. Therefore the missionaries increasingly allowed natives to participate in missionary work. In doing so they anticipated the ultimate objective, namely Africanization and an independent church.

In 1924 the church councils of Blantyre and Livingstonia were united, thus the Church of Scotland was established in Nyasaland. This step was the official confirmation of an independent African church, a symbol of increasing African emancipation. In 1965 the synod of Harare (formerly Southern Rhodesia, today's Zimbabwe) joined the Church of Scotland in Nyasaland, in 1984 the synod of Lundasi (Zambia) did the same, thus creating the Church of Central Africa Presbyterian (CCAP).

Living History

By 1935 most Scottish pioneers had left Africa. Among them was Dr Laws, who in 1927, turned his back on the Dark Continent after 52 years of missionary work. Exhausted, he died soon afterwards in his home country.

In his former residence, the Stone House, which was converted into a museum, some parts of his office and reception room are preserved as he had left them. A picture shows him with a pointed grey beard. On top of his desk lies a tattered Holy Bible, his name Laws written in regular and concise letters. In his desk are his diaries and letters. Although a physician he had very legible handwriting and a precise but elegant writing style. On the wall is his black robe befitting a dignified man of nearly six feet. In the cupboard are a small selection of surveying instruments. Stone House radiates an air of warmth, although the furnishing is practical, without any superfluous items (see *Livingstonia*).

Africanization of Christianity

In the twenties, vacant positions of veteran missionaries were taken up by a generation of young Africans and Europeans. Despite the young blood the Africanization of the CCAP did not take place smoothly. Especially black ministers found that the process moved too slowly. Several groups split off from the CCAP establishing individual churches. One of them, the 'Blackman's Church' still exists in the Tonga region today. The Church of Scotland's missionaries were successful for a number of reasons. Firstly they protected the people they lived with from raiding tribes and merciless slave traders. Furthermore, they became the cherished allies of several chiefs supporting them in their disputes with the British colonial government. (In 1891 Nyasaland became part of British Central Africa, and achieved the status of a protectorate).

Financial power, coupled with religious persistance and energy, plus the fact that the missionaries accepted help with their projects from the natives played an essential part in the success of missionary work. The excellent school system inspired the natives' confidence and induced them to become followers of the Scottish missionaries. Education soon became synonymous with better chances and lucrative employment possibilities. The schools helped to reduce the fear of Christianity. Overton College in Khondowe, Livingstonia, soon gained the reputation of being the best academic school in Central Africa. Those who were rejected had to travel far to receive an education. Dr Banda, Malawi's President, for example. . He was not admitted to Khondowe College and gained academic success in the USA.

By 1959 the synod of Blantyre and Livingstonia had completely taken over the administration from Edinburgh. From then on the CCAP was autonomous, which, however, did not mean that the Scots stopped supporting the CCAP in financial and personnel matters. Even today, every so often red-haired priests are seen flitting across church yards in Blantyre or Livinstonia. They put aside their idea of converting people long ago. The change in the relationship between the white and black church is represented by the slogan 'Interaction Instead of Conversion'. A Malawian priest puts it like this, "There was a time of Christianization in Africa when we were dependent on the help from Europeans. Now the time has come for the Africanization of Christianity, for African songs and prayers, African liturgy and African exegesis."

'FLUE' AND 'BURLEY' IN MALAWI

In a May 1989 issue the Malawian farmer's weekly, *Za Alimi*, played up the annual piece of news: "Here we go again!" In Kanenco, 10 km north of the capital Lilongwe, tobacco auctions are held for weeks on end and champion bargainers from all over the world gather once again. The tobacco industry is to Malawi what the mining industry used to be to Great Britain. In 1986 more than 50% of the export profits came from tobacco sales. Thus the economic future of the coming year depends to a great extent on the outcome of these auctions. Two different qualities are available on the market, the cheaper Flue and the high-class Burley. The latter is particularly popular with the internationally well-known cigarette producers.

Malawian producers are content with the development of tobacco-prices on the world market. Whereas in 1983 the average price for two pounds of tobacco was 2.50 kwacha (US$ 1, £ 0.60), prices doubled during the first auction days in 1989. Malawi is the only country in the world which has not fixed minimum-prices for tobacco. Price fluctuations, even if showing a downward trend, make the annual auctions all the more fascinating and dangerous. The press pays much attention to every price change, regardless of how trivial it might be.

In the auction hall the bales wait for the buyers who walk up and down the halls. Finding the right goods is as hard a job as bargaining for the best prices. With expertise, the buyers, mainly whites, move down the hall using their noses, thumbs and index fingers. The buyers have the sacks undone for them, reach deep into the tobacco and pull out a sample. Moistness, weight, thickness of the leaves, colour and smell determine quality. If tobacco is stored too long or was not thoroughly air or fire-dried it is likely to become mouldy or rotten. It is then worthless.

In 1989 an exceptionally long rainy season damaged the plants: large parts of the country were flooded. The plants lacked time to ripen and the crop time in which to dry. When the auctions opened, buyers instantly complained that the goods were put on the market much too early. Initial demand was low, prices dropped by 20 per cent of the previous year's level. A storm of indignation raced through the papers' headlines: 'Main Source of Foreign Currency Shrinks by Twenty Per Cent.' So Malawi had ten per cent less foreign currency at its disposal.

The Malawian tobacco market is not entirely free from price control thanks to the Growers' Representatives, Mr Mike Underwood for the Flue, and Mr Dick Faasen for the Burley tobacco. After closing time both of them inspect the bales. If prices seem 'unfair' to them, they rip off the price tags and have them declared invalid. The bales which were thought to have been sold are then pushed back on carts into the main storehouse, where the cart pushers dash through the rows with elegance and skill. After two days the same bales will be on sale again. Hopefully they will receive a 'fair' treatment then.

Between the auctions of 1988 and 1989 the block of auction halls situated outside Lilongwe was renovated and extended at great cost. Two and a half millon kwacha were spent on computer equipment, the exhibition grounds were enlarged by an additional 5,000 square metres and two loading platforms with automatic conveyor belts were installed. *Za Alimi* proudly reported that all work at, in and around the auction halls was carried out by Malawian labourers, even the installation of the computers.

By the end of this year's auctions well over 40 million pounds of 'Flue' and 160 million pounds of 'Burley' will have changed hands. That is the equivalent of two billion packets of 50 grammes. Statistically, Malawi provides every second inhabitant of the earth with one packet of tobacco per year.

PART II

The Country Malawi

HISTORICAL ASPECTS

From Nyasaland to Malawi
Before the Europeans discovered the Dark Continent the Africans did not produce any documentation. There are no records in the form of pamphlets, books or minutes of meetings. Thus Nyasaland's history begins roughly with David Livingstone's expeditions in the 1860's. History of this African country starts with the arrival of the whites - what an irony!

Maravi's Discovery by a Missionary
In the year 1863 David Livingstone, a Scottish missionary, had just returned from one of his now world-famous expeditions. His diaries, which were published shortly afterwards, announced to the world that he had followed the Zambezi from the east coast of Central Africa through Portuguese East Africa in 1859. Several hundreds of miles upstream he sailed north on the Shire River which led him through the Shire Highlands, finally arriving at the lake feeding it, Lake Malawi previously known as Lake Nyasa. The region bordering the lake to the east was partially occupied by the Portuguese. The area around the lake was also referred to as Nyasaland. Maravi is a native word meaning 'land of fire'.

In 1884 a British consul was appointed to the districts adjacent to Lake Nyasa to represent the interests of the 32 British citizens living there. By order of the British consul, Buchanan, the Nyasaland Protectorate was established in 1889. The country was placed under protection - without any formal request from the inhabitants - from slave traders and Portuguese conquerors.

The annexation of Nyasaland was part of the long-term objective of British colonial policy: a continuous land bridge between Cairo and Cape Town under British rule. Africa got to know the Christian West on the one hand as religious custodian of the Word of God in Maravi/Nyasaland, and on the other hand as imperialistic protector (tax collectors, judges and settlers).

In 1891 the present frontiers of Nyasaland were established between the Protectorate government and the British South African Company. Neither cared for the violation of tribal territory. At the time the Protectorate was founded four-fifths of Nyasaland's foreign trade was based on the export of ivory. In the course of the country's restructuring, carried out by arriving settlers, the trade in ivory was gradually pushed into the background. Fields were cultivated, first with coffee, then, by way of trial and error, with rubber and cotton. In 1905, when tobacco was grown for the first time, the crop was a great success. In the following years tobacco became the most important cash crop in Nyasaland. This has continued until today (see *Flue and Burley in Malawi*).

Christianisation

Livingstone's discovery and detailed description of Maravi brought about two changes. Livingstone was a Presbyterian missionary of the Church of Scotland. In 1875, more missionaries of his church followed him, conveying a certain concept of life to the natives which the Scottish Malawi expert Shepperson calls the 'habit of historical thinking'. At the General Missionary Conference of Nyasaland in 1910, Dr Elmslie, one of the leading Scottish missionaries in Livingstonia said, "The native thinks our life and institutions were all framed en bloc and were handed over to us in some way, and nothing will awaken him more to the possibilities within the reach of the tribes than to learn the evolution of nations."

He mentioned, as early as 1910, the long-term goal of the natives' emancipation. The missionaries conveyed a social-evolutionary concept to their congregations. English, which was taught in their schools, inevitably united the tribes. Both historical thinking plus the English language were the basis of an integrated political way of thinking.

The second consequence of the discovery of Nyasaland was the cultivation of vast areas of land by white settlers. With his slogan 'Commerce and Christianity', Livingstone helped the white world, that is to say, the West and its nineteenth century representatives to take possession of the area around Lake Malawi. Since slavery was abolished in the USA and cheap African labourers no longer came to work on the plantations, the plantations came to the Africans.

Africa's Close Network of Missions

White settlers and missionaries of different churches sailed to Maravi in the wake of the Scots. In 1861 the Anglican Universities Mission failed. A second attempt to settle on Likoma Island; in 1885 met with success. In the following years the mission also worked on the mainland. A cathedral was built on the island, which today is Likoma's main tourist attraction. Since 1876 the Church of Scotland was established throughout Nyasaland. In 1889 the Dutch Reformed Church followed, with its headquarters in central Nyasaland. The same year the first Catholic mission of the White Fathers arrived. The country is thought to have had the closest network of missions in all Africa. Their importance is acknowledged by President Banda, in effective government since 1966, who considers the Scottish mission to be the foundation of his own party (see *Livingstonia*).

The Chilembwe-Rising of 1915

John Chilembwe was born in Tsangano, a village in the Shire Highlands some time between 1860 and 1871. On the maternal side he was a descendent of the famous chief Kalonga, a fact which added to his prestige. He grew up while his native country was conquered by whites (mainly English and Scots). More than half of the fertile Shire Highlands became white property. The young Chilembwe experienced the gradual disintegration of the traditional agricultural society of his fathers. The inhabitants of Nyasaland lost access to cultivated land and hunting-ground and thereby a great part of their cultural identity.

John went to one of the schools run by the Church of Scotland in Blantyre (named after Livingstone's birthplace east of Glasgow). The contact with Christianity and Bible classes in school were of decisive importance to his future life. In 1892, as a young man, he met the white missionary Joseph Booth by whom he was baptized. From then on he worked together with Booth, and both travelled to the USA to study.

Slavery had been abolished in the USA 30 years earlier. This, together with the shift of racial problems from the political to the social level in the USA clearly influenced Chilembwe's outlook on life. More than ever he felt African. At Providence Industrial Mission he was taught that all men are equal before God. As minister of the Providence Industrial Mission he returned to Nyasaland in 1899.

With financial support from the American Baptists he founded his own mission in his home country in Chiradzulu in the Shire Highlands near Mbombwe. Within a few years, outstations of the mission were established and schools and churches built. The black congregations tilled the soil independently. His mission was successful. Up until the end of 1913 the colonial authorities were pleased with his work in the Chiradzulu Branch of the Providence Industrial Mission. Chilembwe helped the class of under-privileged black people with practical work. By means of education and independent economic activity he laid the foundation for the emancipation of Africans from Europeans. In his writings, published daily, he affirmed that all men are equal and complained about the suppression of Africans in their own country. Most Africans were wage-earners working on someone else's land or tenants of white land owners. They were driven hard in the fields, a tax was imposed on their huts by the British colonial government. Whoever refused to work for the white settlers, often found his hut burnt or his wife taken away until the debt was settled.

Apart from the economic exploitation, Chilembwe, who was familiar with the role of Africans, also noticed sadly the political and legal inequality of his people. In court whites have always right because in the eyes of most white judges, blacks are not human. A further aspect of the deprivation of the natives' human rights was the recruitment of African soldiers for English war purposes, a practice intolerable to Chilembwe. In his opinion, those who were deprived of their rights were not obliged to fight in a war. Accordingly it was clear to him that those who fought side by side in wartime could not be master and slave in peacetime. In the *Nyasaland Times* he asked the government, "Shall we be recognized as being somebody in the best interests of civilization and Christianity after the great struggle is ended? Will there be any good prospects for the natives after the war?"

Reverend Turned Revolutionary
With the outbreak of World War I in 1914, the African continent became also embroiled in the Europeans' war. The problematic nature of the recruitment of African soldiers increased. The colonial

government was in a de facto state of war with its northern neighbour, German East Africa. The policy of suppression and negation of racial problems aimed to create internal peace to support warfare on the frontline. Thus the impact of Chilembwe's writings on the public remained minimal.

In December 1914 Chilembwe's Countrymen met for the first time. Most of them were heads of villages speaking on behalf of a great number of men. They all shared the discontent of being second-class people and they refused to serve in a white army. At several secret meetings they discussed the question of participation in the war and finally agreed that it was better to die in the fight against colonialism than in a colonial war. The uprising was planned, although it was not entirely designed to overthrow the government and the old system.

It was Chilembwe who compared himself to the American martyr John Brown. With his breakneck raid in 1859 Brown wanted to further the liberation of blacks in the United States.

A contemporary of the event, George Simeon Mwase, estimated the number of Chilembwe's soldiers as barely 100 men, organized in four battalions. They were insufficiently trained and armed. From the beginning they did not have a chance against the white army. At the end of the first day of fighting several settlers were killed, but most of the strategic goals had not been met. Traitors among Chilembwe's own ranks warned the whites in advance. The advantage of a surprise attack was therefore lost. From then on the rebels were forced onto the defensive, followed by ten days flight from British soldiers. On the tenth day Chilembwe was shot dead by a British police officer in Mozambique and some of his friends were also killed. Others were arrested and brought to the district prison of the colonial capital Zomba. On February 4, 1915 the Chilembwe Rising ended before it had properly begun.

The Aftermath of the Uprising
The effect of the uprising upon the subsequent period is unclear. For the time being the continuing warfare stabilised the distribution of power. But after the war Nyasaland, earlier than most other British colonies, considered Africanization of the administration, an idea put into practice in the thirties. In 1933 some chiefs were granted an advisory

status in the district administration. In 1955 blacks were, for the first time ever, allowed to enter into government. Surprisingly, we never came across Chilembwe's name in Malawi. Though he was one of the most outstanding historical characters since the discovery of Nyasaland, he remains unsung and forgotten. A popular history book dedicates only three pages to Chilembwe and his uprising. Its tenor is not euphoric and the identification with Chilembwe as 'national' hero is almost non-existent.

Colonial Continuity and New Opposition
In the following decades the position of the colonial masters appeared neither to be weakened nor strengthened. A plan was repeatedly discussed to build a federation of the three states of Nyasaland, Northern Rhodesia and Southern Rhodesia. Eight years after the end of World War II, in 1953, the federation was formed, although Nyasaland was opposed to incorporation, fearing that the two Rhodesia's dominion of white settlers and their policy of racial segregation might spill over into Nyasaland. Once again, black opposition was supported by various Christian missions.

In 1958, Dr Kamuzu Banda, who, from England and Ghana, took part in the foundation of the anti-colonial Nyasaland Congress Party (NCP) returned to Malawi. With his fellow fighter Henry Chipembere he mustered public opinion in a period of world-wide decolonialization. Both were detained, later released from custody and allowed to enter into government.

Independence
Sir Glyn Jones, governor of the Crown in Nyasaland, was the last chief magistrate of the Protectorate of Nyasaland, one of three in British Central Africa. He retired on July 6, 1964, the day when the black, red and green national flag with the rising sun was hoisted for the first time in the former capital Zomba. The new state of Malawi was founded.

Nyasaland, from then on to be known as Malawi, was hardly more than an arbitrary accumulation of land between Tanganyika (later known as Tanzania after the confederation with Zanzibar) in the north, Northern Rhodesia (later Zambia) to the west and Portuguese East Africa in the south. An estimated 4 million people populated the newly independent land of Malawi.

I Never Share Power
Independence meant first of all rearranging the distribution of power. What would new policies look like? Which criteria would determine foreign policy? The administrative machinery had to be set up again.

Dr Banda became Prime Minister, formed a provisional cabinet which would remain in effect for two years until the constitution was laid down. His dependence on Rhodesia, Portuguese East Africa and the Republic of South Africa, all economically successful states, was severely criticized. So was his reform of the regulations covering salary payment of officials and his authoritarian behaviour in general. In the same year, a group of ministers loyal to Banda's former friend Chipembere failed to overthrow him. To avoid detention they escaped abroad. In the third month of independence, on September 8, 1964, Banda spoke in front of parliament. "I will never share power with anybody except with you. If you tell me to go, I will go."

Meanwhile, the home provinces of the banned ministers became a centre of disorder. Banda's answer was to reinforce the troops of the Young Pioneers, the Malawi Rifles and the police, to depose several chiefs and to arrest hundreds of the rebels' followers. In the three following years Banda, who in the meantime became President, endeavoured to reconcile the fronts and at the same time persecuted the stubborn ones. Sporadic purges in the area near Fort Johnston broke the opposition. In May 1965 Chipembere emigrated to the USA. By 1967 Banda's position within Malawi was unassailable. Two years after independence, on July 6, 1966, Malawi gave itself a constitution, from then on calling itself a Presidential Republic. Candidates of only one party run for office during the elections. The President is head of state and head of government, there is neither a vice president nor prime minister.

The One Party State
In 1971 Dr Banda was elected President for life, as of 1977 he has been head of state, head of government, foreign minister, rector of the university, chairman of the only existing party and commander in chief of the forces. Apparently, and according to the constitution, Malawi is a dictatorship. Nevertheless, Banda finds support in his people. The rules of succession are already established in the constitution. Officially an executive committee of the party appoints several candidates from its

own ranks to run for President. So far no potential successor has emerged. The 'Official Hostess', the female representative of the country on Banda's side, is believed to play a major part in the struggle for succession. Recently the name of one of the country's five generals has been mentioned as a possible successor.

Malawi's legislative body consists of a one-chamber parliament whose 110 members belong to the Malawi Congress Party. Furthermore, the President may appoint as many ministers as he likes. On the executive side, the country is divided into three regions composed of districts. At the lowest level the heads of the individual tribes have decisional power. Unlike Zambia, where they also have a national assembly, they only act on a local level. They are appointed and dismissed by the President. The jurisdiction is based both on traditional tribal law and British law.

Policy of Dialogue
Under Banda's rule Malawi is characterized by continuing economic development. It is, and remains, one of the world's poorest countries, but hunger is a phenomenon unknown to Malawi (see *Economic Aspects*).

Regarding foreign policy, the country remains an outsider. Conflicts with the OAU (Organization for African Unity) are frequent. Nairobi airport is sometimes the only one allowing Banda to make a stop over on his journeys to Europe. The reasons for this are his policy of open dialogue with countries such as South Africa, Israel and Taiwan and his good economic relations with former imperialist Portugal together with his anti-communism. He is outspoken against neighbouring countries whom he considers to lack economic pragmatism. Political leaders such as Julius Nyerere (Tanzania) and Kenneth Kaunda (Zambia) belong in this category.

Banda has reason to call himself 'Africa's odd man out', declaring that he would make a pact with the devil if it served his country. Thus it is not surprising that socialist Tanzania recruits guerrilla fighters from the members of LESOMA (Socialist League of Malawi, founded in 1975) and that other opposition activists are granted asylum in Zambia and Mozambique. Depending on how powerful the opposition is, Banda's home policy is either liberal or rigid.

Prospects

The country's immediate future mainly depends on three factors. For one thing, a change in the population policy has to be brought about if Malawi wants to avoid a deficit in the food supply in the near future. The fertile ground has already been cultivated to a large extent, thus an increase in the population leads to a decrease in the average supply. The second variable in the equation is Banda's succession. Both factors are closely connected with one another, as Banda's population policy corresponds so far with that of the Catholic Church.

A third and last point is the development of the country's future external relations. A change is underway in the relationship with South Africa; the situation of the 750,000 Mozambican refugees (1990 level) in the south of Malawi is becoming more and more complicated; the new intellectual affinity with the members of the Frontline States is daring. Malawi, an agricultural country, is dependent on exports and therefore needs a smooth relationship with its trading partners (for recent developments see *Economic Aspects*).

ECONOMIC ASPECTS

Poor British Heritage

Not much of the British economic heritage was left in 1964. Infrastructure and some skilled labourers and teachers were all that was considered indispensable to govern the country. The infrastructure comprised 10,000 km of roads, of which only 400 km were surfaced. 25 years later Malawi possesses 2,000 km of all-year roads, passable throughout the rainy season. By the year 2000 the number of roads is estimated to double, there will be few problems then in transporting agricultural goods quickly over long distances. A functional road and transport system is vital for Malawi's survival. Foreign currency can only be earned by trading Malawi's agricultural produce.

National Income

Almost 40 per cent of the gross national income is produced in the agricultural sector by 80 per cent of the population. Until the beginning of the eighties Malawi's economic growth more than kept pace with the rapid population growth. Ever since then the country has lived through several poor years, gradually exhausting the wealth it had accumulated. The extension of agricultural acreage has reached its limits just as fishing has in Lake Malawi, which so far meets 70 per cent of animal protein demand. The gross domestic product, the equivalent of all goods and services produced in Malawi, has, since 1980, risen from 840 million kwacha to 930 million. Due to the rapid population growth however, the GDP per capita dropped from 139 kwacha to 124 kwacha. According to an international comparison of the GDP, Malawi belongs to the five poorest countries in the world. (At current prices, if the inflation rate is taken into account, the GDP amounts to 337 kwacha per head per year). In 1989 the Minister of Finance, Louis Chimango, presented a draft budget to the national assembly in Zomba primarily aimed at reducing the inflation rate that has risen to over 30 per cent. In 1990 it is to be reduced by 10 per cent by means of various tax reductions, cutbacks in expenditure and a restrictive monetary policy.

In all third world countries taking the gross domestic product as a criterion of an economy's welfare is problematic. It is only a rough indicator and a mere statistical average, which in general glosses over the extent of the deficient money supply. 337 kwacha per year means less than 30 kwacha per month. In dollars this corresponds to the purchasing power of just over US$ 10 on the world market. It is difficult to imagine how anybody can live on this sum. In 1985 the legal minimum wage for an unskilled labourer in Blantyre was one kwacha per day (US$ 0.35; £ 0.25) In the country it was far lower.

Development and Debt of the Model Country

Like the majority of its neighbours Malawi suffers from a high foreign debt. The annual public revenue of 600 million kwacha (US$ 200 million) is confronted with a public debt of about 3 billion kwacha (US$ 1 billion). The national budget is less than twice the local budget of a small town in Europe. Yet Malawi's financial situation is not hopeless. The World Bank, the International Monetary Fund, the European Community and further willing donor countries support the African model country which follows a liberal economic policy. The Federal Republic of Germany alone, as the most important donor country to Malawi, annually pays US$ 30 million in development aid.

External Economy

Foreign trade depends on the value of the raw materials on the international market. Its volume fluctuates with the prices for tobacco, tea, sugar and coffee. 50 per cent of the annual proceeds in exports come from tobacco production. Tobacco producers are happy that prices almost doubled over the last five years (for further information see *Flue and Burley in Malawi*). The fact that the people in Malawi do not starve and go naked, as the President himself put it in his speech at the Independence Silver Jubilee celebrations, is a great success and a phenomenon difficult to explain.

With regards to food supply Malawi takes 13th place out of 50 in Africa, thus is in a better position than most of its neighbours which have far higher gross domestic products per capita. The reason for this might be the great share of subsistence farming whose harvests are only partially considered in the national accounts. Migrant workers are a further factor. In previous decades men moved south to work in South African and Zimbabwean mines to earn hard currency. Depending on the foreign policy and the situation on the home employment market up to 400,000 Malawians regularly worked, and still work, abroad. The foreign currency brought back from South Africa to Malawi helps to finance imports. However, the phenomenon of employment of migrant workers causes several social problems in both South Africa and Malawi. On either side the sexes are unevenly distributed, with the usual consequences.

Classical Education in the Central African Valley

Since independence the number of primary school pupils in Malawi has tripled, the number of those who receive higher education has doubled. The first five years of primary school, which are subject to charges, are compulsory. Since independence the rate of illiteracy has dropped from 80 to 60 per cent. Meanwhile Malawi has its own university with 2,000 enrolled students. The flagship of the Malawian educational system, which is famed beyond the country's boundaries, is the Kamuzu Academy, modelled on a British public school. From all over the country and from neighbouring countries, the elite gather to study Greek, Latin and ancient history.

North Corridor - Last Way Out for Exports

Malawi has no port, yet the country is dependent on the shipment of its agricultural goods. Eight years ago when Mozambique was a peaceful country there were two relatively inexpensive railway connections to the ports of Beira and Nacala. In the course of the civil war practically all Mozambican railway lines were destroyed and Malawi's life-line to the ocean was cut off. Since the road leading through Mozambique to Zimbabwe and on to South Africa is no longer safe for the transportation of goods Malawi has to rely upon a much more expensive means of transportation via the north corridor, a surfaced road which is still under construction. The north corridor leads through the highland area in the north of the country from Kaporo via the Tanzanian town of Kyela to Mbeya. There the goods are transferred on to sealed wagons of TAZARA (Tanzanian-Zambian-Railway) and transported to the port of Dar-es-Salaam. Recently, Malawi was conceded a small area, a free port, in Dar-es-Salaam, from which their goods are shipped to all parts of the world. Malawi's cost of transport is the second highest in the world, due to the costly mode of transportation. The corridor is a mighty project for Malawi. The World Bank, together with the main development aid donor countries, made up a credit and financial package to ensure the financing and construction of this vital trading road. Development aid additionally covers the building of several inland ports on Lake Malawi to transform the lake into the main means of transportation south of Kaporo.

Foreign Trade - Foreign Policy

The reverse flow of trading goods from south to north currently influences Malawian foreign policy. The first official visit of a Tanzanian head of state to Malawi in July 1989 on the occasion of the Independence Silver Jubilee festivities, emphasizes the change in foreign policy. Socialist Tanzania under President Nyerere, who resigned from office in 1985, was not the beloved neighbour of President Banda, who practices a liberal economic policy. In their final statements, voiced on the occasion of the state visit of the new Tanzanian President Mwinyi in July 1989, both sides surprisingly spoke of brotherhood and a single people torn apart by the arbitrary determination of national frontiers established by the colonial power. Both parties tried to point out historical links. The new friend does not mention that the Tanzanian economy benefits from the railway line and the granting of tariff privileges. It was heard in well-informed circles that the new brotherhood is also of financial advantage to Tanzania.

The political price Malawi has to pay is the secession from South Africa, to which it maintained excellent relations until recently (even diplomatic ones) and it had to become an associated member of the league of Frontline States. Countries such as Tanzania, Kenya and

Angola joined the league to get away from economic dependency on South Africa and at the same time to exercise pressure upon it by means of an isolationist policy. South Africans are refused admission to the member countries of the Frontline league. In the future, Malawi is supposed to play the part of a mediator between South Africa and the Frontline States because of its position between the bloc. This opinion was confirmed by the two official visits of Mrs Thatcher and Pope John Paul II in 1989.

GEOGRAPHICAL ASPECTS

Population

According to the 1988 census the Republic of Malawi had 8 million citizens, including 10,000 people of European origin and 4,000 Asians. Since independence a Malawian's average life expectancy has risen by ten years from 35 to 45. Compared to the average life expectancy of a European this is still a shockingly low figure.

As in most developing countries the age structure is pyramid-shaped with a broad base of children under five years of age. On average, the mortality rate of infants and children under five years reaches the incredible figure of 50 per cent. The population increases annually, however, by 4 per cent because of the high birth rate. Traditional thinking still holds that a great number of children increases family prestige. Furthermore, the children help to provide security in old age.

In addition to the 8 million Malawian citizens, 750,000 Mozambican refugees (1990 level) live in UN refugee camps in Malawi. Meanwhile the flood of refugees has ebbed. Those who are already there, however, will stay on for the foreseeable future. They are well looked after, schools and hospitals were built inside the camps where more teachers and medical staff are available than outside the camps. Among the native population jealousy has increased as the refugees apparently have all they need. A great number of Malawians are in a different situation. In 1989 self-sufficient Malawi had to import food for the first time because of the refugees.

The increase in population caused an additional shortage in precious firewood, which, next to waterpower, is the main source of energy in Malawi. Most households still depend on wood for cooking. The difficulty in supporting the Mozambican refugees came together with three major natural catastrophies in 1989 which rocked Malawi's economic equilibrium. Vast parts of the country were flooded during the long rainy season. A hurricane and several earthquakes considerably worsened the situation. Tens of thousands of Malawians became homeless. The government had to ask the Western world for emergency aid which was granted instantly.

No Towns - No Slums

Over 90 per cent of the population lives in rural areas. The remaining 10 per cent, that is to say, about 80,000 people live in towns. Malawi's underdeveloped urbanization is one of the main reasons for an apparently functional social system, according to the motto: no towns - no slums.

On February 1, 1975 sleepy Lilongwe, situated in the central province, with 200,000 inhabitants became the country's capital. The international Kamuzu Airport cannot hide the fact that Lilongwe is neither the most glamorous, nor the biggest town in Malawi. The country's largest town is Blantyre-Limbe in the south. Well over 360,000 people live in this commercial and industrial centre. There is no comparison between Blantyre and modern African industrial towns such as Nairobi or Dar-es-Salaam. Blantyre gives the impression of a cosy, orderly, provincial country town. Nevertheless it is Malawi's unoffficial capital, an opinion also shared by the President. Therefore, the annual Independence celebrations on July 6 are held in the Blantyre Kamuzu stadium.

Malawi, a land-bound country, is surrounded by three countries of quite different political persuasion. To the south and east it borders Mozambique which has been paralyzed by civil war for several years. The socialist FRELIMO government fights right-wing RENAMO rebels. In 1989 a solution was at hand after South Africa had withdrawn its support for RENAMO and the Mozambican government had chosen a reformist course. To the west lies crisis-stricken Zambia under Kenneth Kaunda. The programme for economic reform proposed by the International Monetary Fund causes great suffering for the country. In July 1989 a monetary reform was carried out and the country's borders were closed for two weeks. To the north Malawi has a common border with socialist Tanzania also undergoing economic reforms.

Students create the President's portrait for the Celebration

Lonely baobab in Liwonde Park

Boycotting class

Carrying home firewood

View from Zomba plateau to the north

Lake Malawi near Cape Maclear

Evening on the beach of Golden Sands

Tribes

The exact number of tribes living in Malawi is not known, though all are of Bantu origin. Ever since 1,200 A.D. foreign tribes have migrated to the area around the lake. They can be classified into three main groups of which the Chewa, Yao, Tonga, Ngoni, Nyakusa and Swahili are the most important tribes. Chichewa (language of the Chewa) is the native language of about 50 per cent of Malawians. Furthermore, English, the official language, is a uniting factor.

Most Malawian tribes are matrilineal. This means that hereditary is through the maternal side of a family and the mother makes the choice of residence and other social decisions. The mother's eldest brother has more power over her children than the father of the children. In his role as husband the Malawian man is in a subordinate position. Nevertheless, if he is an eldest brother, he is head of his sister's family fulfilling the important social function of the Mumba, a group of sisters together with their eldest brother, the patriarch. He decides on marriages, the upbringing of his sisters' children according to tribal law and is their representative in legal matters. Successive Mumba of a maternal line form a family: big families are at the centre of a village community.

The fact that tribal constitution is based on a matrilineal structure does not spare the wife from being bound to the house. In every respect she is the pivot of the household, working independently. This independence is at the same time an essential prerequisite for the employment of migrant workers as the women can do without their husbands (see *Economic Aspects*).

Traditional Social Structures in Modern Malawi

Malawian social structure is based on traditional tribal concepts which include chiefdoms, villages and kinship.

Chiefdoms exert the most authority. They exceed the territorial boundaries of a village and they allow one people to have several independent chiefdoms. Almost 200 chiefdoms have been preserved in Malawi to this day. The respective chiefs are granted limited judical powers and administrative functions in certain matters. A chief's wealth and influence usually depends on his number of wives who cultivate the fields, thus enabling him to entertain more guests. His children very often form the nucleus of his followers.

Woman selling herbs in Lilongwe

The village is the next most binding unit. Village boundaries are difficult to establish since the family affinity determines who is part of the village and who is not. Those who marry into a family may remain strangers to the village for the rest of their lives. Religious differences and disputes between families may lead to a divison of the village. The size of a village varies from a handful to hundreds of huts. The villagers are subordinate to the headman, the eldest, who in many cases is related to the chief of the chiefdom. His major task is the assignment of communal land to individual families.

Worship of the forefathers is the most important element of religious life and has at the same time a great impact on everyday life; the ancestors are always asked for advice in questions regarding communal property, because, in essence, the land is only borrowed from them.

The third level of social order is of a family nature. The Chewa, Nyanja, Lombwe and Yao derive their kinship from the maternal side, that is to say, from a man to his sister's sons. In such a **matrilineal** sytem the uncle takes up the position of the father regarding the permission to get married and bride price, etc. The tribes of the Ngonde, Ngoni and Sena are organized in a **patrilineal** way, tracing kinship through the male line. Tumbuka and Tonga have a mixed system of tracing descent. Members of one clan, with the same ancestors, have to observe special regulations, which exclude marriage for example.

Although God, as creator, is worshipped by all natural religions in Malawi, the spirits of the departed play an important role in everyday life. They are perceived as intermediaries between the high God and man. Furthermore, they keep off evil spirits. Thus regular contact with them is essential. The spirits of deceased chiefs are thought to be concerned mainly with matters of community life. Even Christians believe in the significance of ancestors in everyday life. Sorcery and witchcraft are blamed for accidents, illnesses, droughts or sudden wealth. The attitude of the population, especially in rural areas, towards the medicine man or the position of the chief, can only be explained if you try to understand a Malawian's concept of life.

The Languages

Malawi has over a dozen different languages. What seems without order at first sight reveals regularity, if examined closely. The prefix *chi* means language, thus **Chichewa** is the language of the Chewa tribe, the largest language group in the country. As Chinyanja is almost identical with Chichewa, Chichewa became the national language. The Ngoni assimilated major parts of Chichewa. Chilombwe, Chitambuka and Chiyao are further important language groups, each of them spoken by 10 to 15 per cent of the population. The Sena, Khokola, Khonde and Nyakusa each stand for two per cent of the spoken languages. In the north of Malawi a kind of Swahili is spoken. Thanks to a functional school system the number of people who do not speak Chichewa is far below the one million mark. **English** is the official language.

In almost every village you will find somebody who speaks English. Still, some words in Chichewa pronounced by a *nzungu*, a white man, as if by magic, produce a smile on Malawian faces. It shows respect for the country's civilization and is apparently very funny.

The letter 'l' and 'r' are interchangeable. For example, Ndiri is also written Ndili. Malawi and Marave are two different spellings of the same word.

A list of useful words and phrases in Chichewa can be found in the Glossary.

Topography

Lake Malawi, extending over more than 20,000 km^2, the third largest inland lake on the African continent, forms a major part of the border to Mozambique and Tanzania. The Republic of Malawi is situated between the 9th and the 17th south parallel. It streches over 118,484 km^2 which is just under half the size of Great Britain. Lake Chilwa in the south east, Lake Malombe and Lake Malawi cover well over 24,000 km^2 of country. All three have one thing in common; their water level is about 500 metres above sea level. Thus they could be considered mountain lakes.

From north to south the country is cut by the African Rift Valley which in Tanzania splits into the Central and the East African Valley. It is the world's largest superterranean system of valleys. In the northern part of Malawi the African Rift is filled by Lake Malawi, to the south it continues as the Shire Valley. The western edge borders on Zambia and rises to 3,000 metres. Nyika National Park is situated there (see *General Information in Brief*).

Climate

Climatically, Malawi is a transitional country, situated between the humid equatorial area and the subtropical dry zones. Its vegetation is similar to that in a savannah. The country has only three seasons, but climatic zones vary with altitude. The hot and humid rainy season (in Chichewa: dzinja) lasts from the end of November until April, sometimes, as in 1989, even until the first week in June. The rains not only mean you get wet without an umbrella, they also cause a slowing-down in all sectors of life, in flooded areas it even causes a paralyzation. As mentioned before, tens of thousands of people became homeless in 1989 due to flooding. The bad condition of most roads, except for those which are tarmacked, make driving impossible, even with four-wheel-drive.

The second season is the pleasantly dry and cool time from May until August, Southern Hemisphere's winter. It is not free from rain and can be compared to the Central European autumn or spring. During this time of year night frost can occur, while during the day the sun can burn.

At higher altitudes such as Nyika, Zomba and Mulanje, the average annual temperature lies below 18° C. Winter is followed by the dry, hot season lasting from September until November. There is no doubt that the climate is strenuous for a European because of the great fluctuation in temperature with change of altitude (if you travel around) and the atmospheric pressure, which is similar to that during periods of high pressure.

In general the climate is bearable on account of its moderate humidity. Coming from humid East Africa Malawi is a real delight. We recommend the period from June to September as the best time to travel. The rains should definitely be avoided.

PRESIDENT BANDA

Malawi is married to a man called Banda. The roles within this marriage are assigned according to African custom; the husband makes the decisions and the wife does as she is told. The political equivalent of this marriage is the presidential republic which is common in Africa. Generally speaking the presidential republic follows the tradition of a tribal system, that is to say, it is based on the rigid hierarchy of a family, a tribe or a people.

The Country Malawi

According to European democratic understanding somebody who cannot be voted out is not a president. Banda should therefore be called chief, chief of Malawi. Banda is simply there, he was successful once, showed the qualities required of a leader, hence he remains in power.

Banda is about 90 years old (his exact age is unknown). Since 1958 he has appeared wearing sun glasses in almost all official pictures. He takes a serious interest in his people's welfare and contents himself with an army so small it is not worth mentioning, which is indeed a very un-African characteristic. His politics, foreign and economic policy in particular, are not oriented towards unattainable and expensive goals, but toward what is feasible in his country. His personal budget, unlike that of other African leaders, does not overburden the national budget. He manages his affairs by considering pragmatic and social aspects and does not care for ideologies or politically motivated prejudices. Under his control Malawi was the first independent African country to enter into stable relations with South Africa. However, Banda is not in favour of apartheid, this alliance is rather a marriage of convenience. To Malawi, South Africa is a paying country, thus taking a pragmatic and tolerant stance is worthwhile. Until recently 90 percent of exports went through South Africa, 30 percent of imports came from there. Hundreds of thousands of migrant workers from Malawi work in South African mines. Malawian labourers are welcome in South Africa because they are hard-working, cheap and do not interfere with South African politics. Malawi has always welcomed South African tourists and, until recently, was one of the few independent African states to allow them entry into the country.

Banda's Biography

A historian who analyzed Malawian history wrote, "the story of Dr H. Kamuzu Banda is the political history of Malawi." Thus it seems appropriate to outline the life of Dr Banda though information about him is scarce.

Having studied different sources I found he was born shortly before the turn of the century near Kasungu. He was granted the privilege of education, learning how to read and write at the mission school of Mtunthama, founded in 1905, where lessons were held in the shade of a Kachere tree. Banda, being the best pupil in the class, was sent to the mission school of Chilanga. He failed, however, to make the great leap forward to the elite school of the missionaries of the Church of Scotland in Kondowe, Livingstonia. He thus lost his only chance to receive further education in his own country. The young Banda's life was shaped at the age of fourteen when the pursuit of academic credits led him through Mozambique and Rhodesia to South Africa. Banda had to walk a thousand miles through more or less unexplored territory where a couple of years previously a great number of missionaries, taking part in an expedition, had lost their lives.

Yet Banda made his way. He left his family and arrived in Hartley (Southern Rhodesia), half way to South Africa, where he worked in a hospital. Soon he moved on to the Transvaal where he became a miner in Witwaterstrand, trying to save up money for passage to the USA.

Although there were signs of political emancipation for the black population in his homeland, finally resulting in the Chilembwe Rising of 1915, Banda decided to follow his academic career. He did not return to his native country for nearly four decades.

It is unknown how Kamuzu Banda, a black foreigner, managed to study at a university in the United States in the twenties. Despite their policy of racial segregation and being in the grip of an economic depression, he still succeeded. He started studying at the Wilberforce Academy in Ohio and took his Bachelor's degree in philosophy when he was 31. In 1937, at the age of 40, he took a medical doctor's degree at the Mehaarrary College in Nashville, Tennessee. With the degree in medicine the dream born in Hartley (Southern Rhodesia) had come true.

He moved again, this time from the USA to Great Britain to continue his studies at the famed University of Edinburgh in Scotland. There he came to know the Presbyterian Church of Scotland which had already set up a great number of missions in Malawi. He even became an 'elder' of his congregation. With the outbreak of World War II in 1939 he moved to Liverpool, later to North Shields where he opened a surgery. After the war he decided to move his surgery to London. The London period was of great importance to Banda, now fifty years old. He encountered Africans who were fighting for independence in exile. Slowly he developed his own idea on the liberalization of his people from colonialism. These years of non-academic education drove the ageing Banda back to his homeland. He became friendly with Mzee Jomo Kenyatta (Kenya), Kwame Nkruhma (Ghana), and Julius Nyerere (Tanzania) who were soon to play a part in the 'African fight for independence on the international political stage'. These men sharpened his mind to the real situation in Africa. Although he had taken an interest in the politics of Nyasaland in the early thirties, he did not take any political action until the early fifties. It was then that he formed the Nyasaland African Congress (NAC), a nationalist and anti-colonial organization. He advocated that both Rhodesias (today's Zimbabwe and Zambia) and Nyasaland should remain autonomous. For a time his plan was thwarted when, in 1953, a Federation of these countries was established. His commitment to Nyasaland was not in vain.

A functional organization concerned with both nationalist and political matters was born. Banda became one of its leaders. In 1953 Banda returned to Africa to work and live there for the first time since his youth. Before he finally went home, he set up a surgery in Ghana, where he had the opportunity to study the mistakes made by the young independence movement there. On his arrival in Nyasaland on July 6th, 1958 his followers gave him a warm welcome.

He intensified his activities against the federation with the Rhodesias, gathering round him those chiefs of individual tribes who, like himself, dreamt of abolishing the colonial government. In 1959 he was arrested together with 1,500 of his supporters. During his twelve months detention he developed the political concept of the Malawi of his dreams. Shortly after his release Banda set up the Malawi Congress Party (MCP), meant as a replacement for the banned NAC. He planned to hold the office of Chairman of the party for life.

In the early sixties Britain, together with other colonial powers, changed their colonial policy. Colonialism and Imperialism were on the verge of defeat. In the sixties African independence came true. The colonial powers looked for peaceful ways to back out of their responsibility. In Malawi Dr Banda was thought to comply with Britain's wishes. After the partially free election of 1961 he became a member of both the government and the Legislative Council. In 1963 he was the first African in central or southern Africa to become president. Nyasaland became officially independent on July 6, 1964, from then on calling itself Malawi. Exactly the same day two years later, Malawi was proclaimed a republic and given a constitution. The sixth of July, the day of Banda's return, independence and foundation of the republic, was declared a national holiday. In 1971 Banda's right to lifelong presidency was laid down in the constitution - as chief of Malawi for life.

Pragmatism in the Name of God

Banda's policy is primarily pragmatic. Since South African ports, vitally important to inland Malawi, are not accessible any more on account of the civil war in Mozambique, Malawi has shown a great interest in neighbouring Tanzania.

Tanzania, however, is a member of the Frontline States, a league whose declared policy is simply to boycott South Africa and to ban all South Africans from entering the member countries. Tanzania has what Malawi needs, a railway line running from the Malawian border to the port of Dar-es-Saalam. Though it has appeared that Banda was turning his back on South Africa in reality he was only ensuring the economic survival of his own country.

It is now clear why President Mwinyi from Tanzania was the most important guest of honour at the 25th anniversary celebrations of the Republic of Malawi. The socialist neighbour has even been promoted to the rank of a sister nation and South Africa regarded as a dictatorial country. Overnight a number of previously banned books, ranging from Mandela to Biko, were put on sale. In return for this political lip service Malawi is allowed to transport goods through Tanzania without paying customs. Furthermore, Malawi is granted a free trade zone in the port of Dar-es-Saalam. Thanks to Banda, Malawi is the first land locked African country with a free port on the Indian Ocean.

The president is highly moral and cares for good manners, anyone using bad language in public is fined, men are requested to wear short hair (the ears must not be covered). The Malawi tourist is also expected to respect these requirements. Women's knees must be covered by a skirt, non complicity may result in being taken to the nearest police station. Trousers for women are taboo. The man responsible for these rules is President Banda himself (see *General Information in Brief*). In October 1989 the MCP announced that Malawians are no longer allowed to beat their wives. Banda allegedly said, "Kamuzu is husband to all Malawian wives." And who would dare to slap the president's wife?

Regarding domestic policy, the country is rigidly organized; corruption, which is common elsewhere is unknown in Malawi. The state machinery apparently works well. The only official party is Banda's Malawi Congress Party and trade unions are under control of the Malawi Trade Union Congress. Industrial action is illegal. The only opposition movement operates in exile from Lusaka (Zambia) and Dar-es-Saalam. Whether it is significant is hard to tell for its actions so far have not met with success.

Key to Banda's Personality

The key to Banda's personality is Christian belief. During the Pope's visit to Malawi in May 1989 the whole country was wild with joy. When John Paul II and the President finally met, the stern and severe Banda burst into tears, kissed the Pope's hands and embraced him.

Having been brought up and educated in a mission school and worked as an 'elder' in a congregation of the Church of Scotland, he is familiar with and fascinated by the Christian West. He watches his people's morals, caring for the poor and the homeless, preaching charity and diligence, converting disbelievers.

BLANTYRE

- Ⓢ Street vendor
- Ⓚ Cinema
- Ⓟ Post office
- Ⓗ Train station
- Ⓑ Bus station
- Ⓒ St. Michael and all Angels Church
- Ⓣ Town Hall
- Ⓡ Ryalls Hotel
- Ⓜ Mt. Soche Hotel

Grace Bandawe Conference Centre

Museum, Stadium, Limbe

PART III

Travel Guide

GENERAL INFORMATION IN BRIEF

Behaviour
In public you have to behave yourself, which means do not use bad language, don't criticise the President or the country. Men must wear short hair (the ears must not be covered) and women are not allowed to wear trousers. Skirts have to cover the knees fully. Bribing officials is not advisable.

Business Hours

Banks	Mondays to Fridays 8.00 to 13.00
Shops	Mondays to Fridays 8.00 to 17.00
	Saturdays 8.00 to 12.00
Offices	Mondays to Fridays 7.30 to 17.00
	lunch break 12.00 to 13.00

Note: Some offices are closed to the public in the afternoon.

Climate
Malawi's climate is temperate like that prevailing in equatorial areas and subtropical dry zones. The vegetation is similar to that of the savannahs. Due to the topography climate and vegetation vary according to the elevation. Average annual temperature in the plains is 22°-32° C, highest temperature about 39° C, lowest temperature about 14° C. Average temperature in the highlands is 13°-27° C.

Diplomatic Missions of Malawi

Great Britain
Malawi High Commission
33 Grosvenor Street
London W1X ODE

Canada
Malawi High Commission
7 Clemow Avenue, Ottawa
Ontario K1S 2A9

South Africa
Malawi Embassy
PO Box 11172
Brooklyn, Pretoria 0011
R.S.A.

USA
Malawi Embassy
Bristol House
1400-20th Street N.W.
Washington D.C. 20036

Zimbabwe
Malawi High Commission
42-44 Salisbury Street
Harare
Zimbabwe

Malawi Mission to the United
Nations
767 Third Avenue, 8th floor
New York, NY 10017
USA

Diplomatic Missions in Malawi

Great Britain
High Commission
PO Box 30042
Capital City, Lilongwe
USA

Embassy of the United States of
America
PO Box 30166
Capital City, Lilongwe 3
Tel. 730369

Economy
Malawi's economy is market-oriented and self-sustaining. There have been no hunger catastrophes although the population has been increasing steadily.

Currency
The monetary unit is the kwacha. 1 kwacha = US$ 0.35; £ 0.25 (1990)

Entry Regulations
Visas are not needed for members of the British Commonwealth, the USA, South Africa and some European countries such as Federal Republic of Germany. Exceptions are Austria, France, Italy, Spain and Switzerland. For details inquire at your embassy.

Traveller's cheques and cash must be declared on entry to the country. The amount of 20 kwacha may be brought in. You must possess adequate funds for your length of stay and a return ticket. **Books**, except for diaries, are likely to be confiscated. A **vaccination card** must be shown, vaccination against **yellow fever** must be obtained if arriving from an endemic area. Your local doctor should know the present situation.

Getting There
There are two possibilities. By land via Tanzania (the route Mbeya, Kyela, Kaporo, Karonga) or from Zimbabwe across the transit road through Mozambique (a dangerous route because of the civil war). By plane direct to the capital Lilongwe (for flight connections see *Transport*).

Health
Hospitals are in Livingstonia, Muzuzu, Lilongwe (Likuni Hospital) and Blantyre (see *Health*).

Historical Summary
Nyasaland became a British Protectorate in 1891. The Chilembwe Rising took place in 1915. In 1953 Nyasaland joined with Southern and Northern Rhodesia Central Africa federation. This federation was broken up in 1963 by the Nyasaland African Congress Party under Banda. Nyasaland gained independence from the British crown in 1964 and shortly afterwards Banda became President of the newly named Malawi.

Inhabitants
About 8 million friendly people, belonging to a dozen different tribes live in Malawi. Additionally about 14,000 non-Africans live here, among them 10,000 North Americans and Europeans. The rate of population growth is 4 per cent.

At the beginning of 1990, 750,000 Mozambican refugees lived in camps in the south of the country. About 800,000 Malawians live abroad, mainly in Zimbabwe and Zambia. Approximately 15,000 work in South African mines.

Language
The national language is Chichewa, official language is English. You can get by with English, even in remote places.

Media
The Daily Times is an English language newspaper, the Malawi News and Malawi Gazette are weeklies. Monthly magazines are written in Chichewa. International newspapers arrive at least one day later. Malawi has no TV station.

National Holidays

January 1	New Year's Day
March 3	Martyr's Day
May 14	Kamuzu Day
July 6	Republic Day
1st Monday in August	Bank Holiday
October 17	Mother's Day
December 21	Planter's Day
December 25-27	Christmas holidays
movable holidays	Good Friday, Easter Sunday and Monday

Often additional holidays are announced on Republic Day.

Neighbours
Zambia to the north west, Tanzania to the north and north east, the rest borders on Mozambique (see *Geographical Aspects*).

President/Government
Malawi is a presidential Republic and member of the Commonwealth. The President for Life, Dr Hastings Kamuzu Banda, is head of a one-man-government. Malawi is a totalitarian state which is perfectly safe for tourists, provided they respect the country's rules.

The **flag** consists of three horizontal stripes in black, red and green with a red rising sun in the centre.

Prices
Prices vary in different regions. Hot snacks are a lot cheaper than a meal at McDonald's. However, eating out in restaurants costs the same as in Europe. Prices for accommodation are comparable to Western standards. Transportation costs are less. Hospital care (without treatment) costs about US$ 25 (£ 18) per day (as a private patient with full board).

Geography
The country is approximately the size of Portugal, 118,500 km^2, with the inland lakes accounting for 24,000 km^2 (the greatest among them is Lake Malawi). From north to south the country spans 840 km, from east to west 80 to 160 km.

Telephone
Making calls from public call boxes may be problematic. International calls should be made from the telephone exchange or major hotels.

Time of Travelling
The dry season lasts from May to October. Average humidity is 85 per cent in the mornings and 40 per cent in the afternoons. During the rainy season (November - April) it rises between 70 and 100 per cent. July is the coolest month, with average temperatures varying from 10° to 22° C. The most convenient time for travelling is from June to October.

Tourist Information
The Malawi Department of Tourism, PO Box 402, Blantyre, regularly publishes a booklet of about 20 pages, obtainable free of charge.

Further addresses
Malawi Tourist Office
33 Grosvenor Street
London W1X ODE

What to Wear
Casual summer clothes in light cotton for the savannah and the lake shore, woollen clothes and rain gear for the highland areas.

Women must not wear trousers, and skirts must cover the knees. Straw hats and light skirts, which may be worn instead of European-style clothes by women, are obtainable in Malawi. Emphasis is placed upon proper evening wear in hotels or for official occasions.

TRANSPORT

The railway in this mountainous country is of minor importance. The only existing railway line runs in the south, from Blantyre via Salima to Lilongwe. The railway network comprises 790 km. Access to the ports of Beira and Nacala has been cut since the outbreak of civil war in Mozambique. For centuries Lake Malawi has not only been the main source of fish, but also the most important communication link in the country. A number of cargo boats are used to cover long distances from one end of the lake to the other whilst the picturesque dugouts are still used on short distances.

By Train

Travelling by train is a worthwhile experience. The carriages seem to belong to the days of old. Third-class passengers are crammed together on bare wooden benches. Second class compartments have sparingly-covered clean wooden benches, well spaced to chat with fellow travellers. It is the speed of the train which makes the journey so attractive; the villages with children waving, fields, mountains and animals appear in slow motion. Even with the camera permanently ready you will be unable to record all the countless impressions (for information contact Malawi Railways, tel. 642244)

By Ship

There is no doubt that the most wonderful and most typical form of transport are the two steamers on Lake Malawi, passenger ships with the pleasant sounding names of **Ilala** and **Mtendere**. Twice a week they travel the distance from **Monkey Bay** in the south, past **Likoma Island** to **Chilumba**, a trip which takes three days. While in Monkey Bay a gangway leads on board, passengers and freight are carried in overloaded lifeboats at other stops. A small fleet of dugouts provides the steamers with fruit, fish, pastries etc. To those who would like to make the complete journey we recommend booking first-class cabins which are good value for money.

The steamers are multi-functional, serving as an inexpensive means of transport for the poor, substitute for a luxury liner for the rich tourist, as a connecting line to Likoma Island and other remote places and as a means of transport for all kinds of goods.

The Ilala

The Ilala, named after the village where Livingstone died, is the older and rustier, the bigger and better-known of the two ships. Our journey on the Ilala remains unforgettable. The steamer was overcrowded as always and Lake Malawi, normally very calm, was churned up like an ocean. It was hard to imagine we were on an inland lake. The Ilala all of a sudden seemed small and vulnerable, pitching and tossing in the waves until space to lean over the rail was scarce. In the fresh air of the foredeck we found a pile of cardbord boxes where we thought we could at least stretch out and get an hour's sleep. What a mistaken idea! The dancing stars above seemed as if they would fall down any minute, but the worst came from the boxes below us, the stench of rotten fish. Days after that experience on the foredeck the smell was still in our clothes and noses. But travelling the lake is not always that tough. When the cargo is bananas or maize the trip is much more pleasant! As the third and second class are almost identically uncomfortable we recommend travelling first class.

How different life is on the upper deck! One passenger has the same amount of room at his disposal as several families together with the cattle has on the other decks. The first class offers comfortable beds, hot showers, friendly service, spacious cabins, seven-course dinners and last but not least two bars with a good selection of drinks and panoramic view of the lake. Sunny days on deck and romantic starry nights ensure a pleasant journey. As the cabins are very often fully booked it is advisable to make reservations at least two months in advance. Otherwise there is always room to sleep under the stars on the upper deck where you can enjoy cleanliness and good meals.

The Mtendere: For Backpack Travellers
The Mtendere only has a third and a second-class deck, the latter being neither crowded nor luxurious. On the route from Monkey Bay to Likoma Island the main deck of the Mtendere turns into a meeting-place for a dozen backback tourists on their way to the Islands. A place to have a chat, exchange addresses and to sleep wrapped up in a warm sleeping bag. The next morning everybody is covered with soot particles from the chimney and a bit stiff from sleeping on the bare planks.

Meals on the second- and third-class decks of both the Mtendere and the Ilala are plain but good and inexpensive (chambo with rice costs 1.25 kwacha, beef and chips cost 2.50 kwacha). Please note that hygienic conditions in the toilets of the lower decks on both ships are very poor.

Information from Malawi Railways, PO Box 5144, Limbe, tel. 652244

Timetable
Timetables are reasonably reliable, though departures may be delayed by loading or unloading cargoes. To compensate there is always a long stop at Nkhata Bay.

Read the second column for each boat from the bottom to the top. Times are different over the Easter holiday period.

Place & Time of Departure

Harbours	Ilala North	Ilala South	Mtendere North	Mtendere South
Monkey Bay	Fr 8.00	---	Tu 10.00	---
Chilinda	Fr 10.30	We 15.30	---	---
Makanjila	Fr 14.00	We 12.00	---	---
Chipoka	Fr 21.30	We 8.00	Tu 22.30	Mo 6.30
Nkhotakota	Sa 6.00	Tu 17.00	We 6.30	Su 14.30
Likoma Island	Sa 13.30	Tu 10.00	We 13.00	Su 8.00
Chizumulu Island	Sa 16.00	---	We 14.30	Su 6.00
Nkhata Bay	Su 4.00	Tu 3.00	Th 6.00	Su 2.30
Mwangwina Bay	---	---	Th 7.30	Sa 16.30
Usisya	Su 7.30	Mo 13.30	Th 9.30	Sa 13.30
Ruarwe	Su 9.30	Mo 11.30	Th 11.00	Sa 13.00
Charo	---	---	Th 12.00	Sa 11.00
Mlowe	Su 12.30	Mo 8.30	Th 14.30	Su 8.30
Chitimba	Su 14.30	Mo 6.30	---	---
Chilumba	---	Mo 4.00	Fr 6.00	Sa 6.00
Kambwe	---	---	Fr 10.30	---
Kaporo	---	---	Fr 12.30	---

By Bus

Buses are cheap, quite reliable and fast. In almost all major towns the tourist has a choice of two kinds, **express** and **local buses**. Travelling express does not strain a European budget, and is a lot more comfortable and faster, especially on longer journeys as stop-overs are less frequent. Nevertheless it is a strenuous trip. Five people are seated in one row on badly covered wooden benches which make you feel every hole and bump in the road. Malawian roads are better than those of some neighbouring African countries, though there are still many untarred. Not only the roads put your fondness of travel to the test, but also the heat, dust and the lack of space. However the constantly changing scenery of the deep-blue lake, mountain ranges and traditional villages with their four and two-legged inhabitants make up for the inconveniences.

The main bus stations are never far from the town centres. It is advisable to buy tickets in advance, if possible. Seats cannot be reserved.

Join a queue and make for a seat. If possible take your baggage with you into the bus. The luggage rack on top of the bus is safe for rucksacks (suitcases are less convenient) but is exposed to the fine red dust, which will have completely covered your luggage by the end of the journey. If you do not get a seat you may comfort yourself with fruit and sweets offered by young Malawians through the window at each and every stop. Specialities vary according to region, in the north you find Samosas, in the south different types of sweet cakes.

Car-Rental

We highly recommend renting a car to those who can afford it, to make full use of the 2,500 km of all-year roads. During the rainy season a third of the non-surfaced roads are impassable, even with four-wheel drive. This applies essentially to the swamp areas (dambos) around Lilongwe and the Lake Chilwa plain. An **International Driving Licence** is essential for renting a car. There is a minimum age requirement which varies at each agency. At first sight car rental prices seem high. National Parks, however, are not accessible without a car and prohibited for pedestrians. The only exception to this rule is Nyika Game Park which allows its visitors to walk about freely. If you watch out for special offers and compare prices you should be able to rent a car for a couple of days. Rucksack tourists can join a group to rent a minibus. With a bit of luck you will always find congenial travellers, but be aware of cheats. Some people do not pay their share at the end of a trip. Some car agencies might try to claim damage from you which was in fact caused by the previous driver. Our personal experience with car rental always proved reliable, though prices did not always correspond to the type of car advertised.

Book in advance from the airports or major hotels or in Blantyre, Mzuzu or Lilongwe. By the way, the additional charge for a driver is minimal, a small sum per day plus meals. You find the best selection of car rental services in Blantyre. **Insurance** is not included in the rental price, full comprehensive coverage is rarely possible. In any case, insurance matters ought to be settled beforehand.

Traffic Rules

Driving is on the left. Wearing seat belts is compulsory if the car is equipped with belts. The sound of the horn is heard frequently, it has to be blown before overtaking a car. The **speed limit** in small towns and villages is 46 km/h, on country roads 80 km/h, in Blantyre and Lilongwe 64 km/h. Radar traps do not exist, they are, however, effectively substituted by pothole traps. Driving in the dark should be avoided because the roads remain busy throughout the night. People walking, cars driving with full head-lights and the potholes will give you a difficult time.

By Plane
Domestic flights (airports exist in Lilongwe, Blantyre, Karonga and Mzuzu) are scheduled twice a week, a ticket costs about US$ 100. Except for the seats being too close together, the twin-engined aircrafts of Air Malawi meet European standards. Often an airport consists only of one single runway for take-offs and landings and a tiny hall for arrivals and departures. Primarily Malawian businessmen and politicans travel by plane. There are no students' reductions on normal tariffs.

International Flights: Getting to Malawi
Since 1983 all international air traffic lands at Kamuzu Airport, 13 miles from Lilongwe. Direct flights to Malawi are offered by:

- Ethiopian Airlines, via Addis Abeba (recommended, Africa's most modern fleet with the new Boeing 767);
- KLM, via Amsterdam;
- Kenya Airways, via Nairobi;
- UTA, from Paris, Lyon, Marseille, Nice (French airline);
- Zambia Airways, via Luanda, from Brussels, Zurich, Vienna.

In Britain there are several agencies that specialize in Africa. These include **STA** which is in the forefront of Africa know-how and an excellent source of information for independent travellers as well as cheap flights. STA has branches in the UK in London, Cambridge, Oxford, Bristol and Manchester, in Australia and across the USA, and caters for anyone looking for an inexpensive flight or interesting tour. STA has many branches; their Africa Desk is at 117 Euston Rd, London NW1 2SX, tel. 071 388 2266. Two of the many US branches are: 17 East 45th St, suite 800, New York, NY 10017; tel. 212 986 9470. 7204 Melrose Ave, Los Angeles, CA 90048; tel. 213 934 8722.

Trailfinders is another company with long experience in helping independent travellers. They have a library, a vaccination centre, and an insurance scheme - in fact everything you need under one roof. Trailfinders, 42-48 Earls Court Rd, London W8 6EJ, tel. 071 938 3366.

Wexas offers the combination of economical flights and low-priced tours in their 'Discoverers' programme (together or separately) and travel insurance. 45 Brompton Rd, London, SW3 IDE, tel. 071 584 8113.

The **Africa Travel Centre** is probably the expert on all aspects of travel to and in Africa, and catering specially for the independent traveller or small groups, ATC offer some unusual - and tempting - options, such as self-drive cars, excess baggage and freight forwarding (ideal for expeditions). 4 Medway Court, Leigh St, London WC1H 9QX, tel. 071 387 1211.

Africa House in London provides any age group with inexpensive airline tickets to Malawi.

Return prices from London start at about £ 650, from Paris at about £ 550 and from Frankfurt at about £ 600.

EQUIPMENT

This is a list of items we found useful in Malawi. What you take with you depends on your budget, destination, duration of the journey, and where you plan to stay. A list can therefore never be complete. It helps to make your own while preparing for the journey.

The Medical Kit
Some adventurers travel to Malawi with their passport, traveller's cheques, cash and a tooth brush. In the chapter *Health* dangers of such an attitude are pointed out. It is advisable to take a carefully planned medical kit, which is of far greater value than its actual price. It should thus be stored in a breakproof, air-tight plastic or aluminium box at the bottom of your rucksack or suitcase, safe from robbery, heat, damp, dust and vibrations.

Luggage
If you plan to stay in top-class hotels take a suitcase, otherwise a **backpack**. Even a single stay in a National Park for a couple of days makes it necessary to have a rucksack. Regardless of the advantages of

modern **frameless backpacks**, they cannot be secured around a bedpost or tied to each other. The weight of a backpack should not exceed 9 - 12 kilos. Water and food supplies plus souvenirs will add to this basic weight as soon as you are in the country. Airline regulations set a weight-limit of 20 or 25 kilos. If possible, pack medicines, maps and camera equipment in an extra bag as hand-luggage.

What To Wear

For hotel guests evening wear is a must. One evening dress or a light cotton suit is sufficient. The backpack tourist who every now and then might like to avail himself of air-conditioning, swimming pool, good service, restaurant, telephone and good sanitary arrangements, should bring along one set of adequate clothes.

Light cotton trousers and shirts with long sleeves protect against the sun, mosquitoes and cool evening winds. **Sturdy shoes**, which must be worn-in, are useful for hiking and protect against snakes and scorpions. A pair of **sandals** for the beach and less-than-clean bathrooms should not be forgotten. A hat is essential, but can be bought as a souvenir in Malawi. **Woollen clothes** are indispensable. A simple **rain-proof jacket or poncho**, which may serve as both protection from the sun and rain and as a waterproof sheet, is sufficient.

Imposed Fashion: Skirts

Women have to wear skirts fully covering the knees, trousers are taboo for them. Tourist places such as the beaches of Lake Malawi and hotels are exempt from the regulation. If you violate it, you might be rebuked, or even arrested. Bring woollen tights for cool hours. *Khangas*, the colourful materials worn by African women and sold everywhere, are multi-functional; they are used as bags, scarves, nappies, prams and dresses. Any street tailor will make you a fine skirt out of them.

Hair

Men too must respect Malawis regulations. Hair must be worn short, not covering the ears. The airport hairdresser will make sure you comply with the rules.

Camping gear

An igloo-tent has the advantage that no tent pegs are necessary. The inner tent must be mosquito-proof, the bottom waterproof. A warm

sleeping bag (suitable for temperatures as low as 0° C) and a sleeping mat are essential.

A cooking stove is essential if you are camping but is also useful for any budget traveller. For the latest stoves on the market visit a good backpacking shop - the YHA ones are excellent, phone 0784 458625 for the address of your nearest branch. Bear in mind that Camping Gaz cannisters are not available in Malawi and may not be carried on aircraft. Gasolene and paraffin are widely available in Malawi.

Checklist
air ticket
passport; visas if required
traveller's cheques
cash (in dollars or pounds Sterling, change the money in Malawi)
credit cards (Diner's Club, American Express)
international certificate of vaccination
insurance certificates
international driving licence
student identification card
copies of documents and traveller's cheques
money bag or belt
list of official currency operations
diary, packed watertight, with a list of addresses (e.g. number of whom to contact in case of emergency)

medical kit (see *Health*)
any necessary prescriptions for glasses or medication
malaria preventives
sunglasses

clothes (see above)
swimming costume
items of body care (soap should be non-polluting)
pocket mirror
towel, may be replaced by a *khanga*
sewing gear

sleeping bag
sleeping mat or air mattress

tent
sheet (for use in budget hotels or as sun-protection)
small camping cooker
aluminium pot (very cheap in Malawi)
deep aluminium plate (replaces a pan); cup

water container
compass
binoculars
maps

matches, disposable lighter
a small torch
plastic bags
strong padlock and chain
wire (to repair rucksack, grill fish, etc)
nylon string (see *Likoma Island*)
adhesive tape
photo equipment

MONEY MATTERS

Though rates of exchange and prices vary from month to month we hope that our information is nevertheless useful to you. Malawi's monetary unit is the **kwacha** (meaning cock) which is worth US$ 0.35/£ 0.25. One kwacha has 100 **tambalas**, 10 tambalas make 1 shilling and 2 shillings are one **florin**.

We cannot give the reader a golden rule of how much money the average tourist spends in Malawi, simply because we did not meet the average tourist and therefore could not ask him. We also have to refute the rumour that one can live on a couple of pennies, that is to say, a couple of tambalas in Malawi. If you expect accommodation of European standard be prepared to pay the price. On the other hand, the visitor who is willing to live on local dishes of fish and the traditional corn mush known as *Nsima* (called Ugali in East Africa, Mielie in South Africa), rice and fruit and furthermore sleeps under the open sky can live on a couple of kwacha a day. The greatly varying transport prices are a major cost factor. Hitch-hiking is not always possible. Travelling by bus is feasible with two-figure sums but costs nerves and intervertebral discs. Rented cars are expensive, especially those of better quality. Malawi looks tiny on the map, but a tour through a country whose greatest inland lake stretches over half the size of Great Britain takes a long time. A third-class steamer tour on Lake Malawi costs a tenth of the first-class ticket.

A Malawi holiday costs the same as in other Central African countries. Please note that admittance to Malawian national parks is inexpensive. Calculate on spending roughly the same amount as you would at home.

In case of accidents or illness you should have additional financial means with you to pay for the hospital or return transport. Even if your insurance company later reimburses you for the damage, you are expected to pay cash.

Money Tips

It is essential to keep your **currency declaration** in order, to see that the bank registers every foreign exchange operation on the sheet. The authorities may react harshly to fraud. If customs officers have reason to be annoyed, bribery is in vain. We advise you not to change foreign currency illegally. The profit gained is not worth the risk involved. Luxury goods (mainly cameras and accessories, lately there was a great demand for computer diskettes) are worth a lot more than at home, but the selling of such goods is also illegal.

If your currency declaration is incorrect do not try to fake it. Absent-minded tourists who lose their declaration or throw it away without thinking will find that Malawian officials deserve their reputation of being friendly and obliging. Our advice: honesty is the best policy. Malawian prisons are rougher than those in Britain.

Precautions against Theft

Banks take US dollars and pounds Sterling. It is best to carry money in the form of traveller's cheques. Shortly before departure small cheques should be at hand to avoid having to change a large sum of kwacha which are almost worthless at home.

A money bag worn around the neck (fortified with wire) or belt around the waist are old but proven hiding places for valuables. Notes and cheques can be hidden in the frame of the backpack, inside the shoes underneath the inner sole or sown into a jacket. It is important to protect the papers from sweat and damp by wrapping them in plastic; choose at least three different hiding places. An old purse with a few bills inside draws attention away from the place where you keep the bulk of your money. It is useful to have a couple of coins in your trouser pocket to pay for small items without showing big notes.

Receipts of traveller's cheques should be kept in a safe place; it is best to copy them and to write down the numbers of drawn cheques. The same applies to your passport, vaccination certificate, receipts of valuables etc. Although Malawi is a safe country, except for the area around Nkhata Bay where robberies have been reported, valuables should be carefully looked after. A normal camera is the equivalent of several years' income for a well-paid Malawian. We learned that pocket cameras or special camera belts are a good solution, leaving your hands free.

Camera equipment, like other valuables, is relatively safe in Malawi. Street robbery, pick-pockets, hotel burglaries and stealing on the beaches are still little known vices in Malawi. Partly because tourism is a recent phenomenon, but also because Malawians respect their fellow men and do not consider the lack of wealth reason to steel. Coming from Kenya, Tanzania or even Mozambique, a pleasant difference will be noticed in people's attitudes. Repeatedly, items such as a ball-point pen or an empty bottle, which we had left behind, were handed back to us. We trusted people's honesty, yet the visitor should not tempt others by leaving his belongings around. Even an inexpensive camera is the equivalent of several years' income for many Malawians.

The greatest thieves in Malawi are monkeys at Cape Maclear and ravens in the Nyika Park, with the latter being the greediest, nothing is safe from them!

HEALTH

Facts about Malaria

Malaria is transmitted by the bite of the female **Anopheles mosquito**. The Plasmodium parasite first attacks the liver, then the red blood corpuscles, which are destroyed in batches. Their destruction results in fits of fever occuring regularly or sporadically, depending on the type of malaria. Further symptoms are headache, weakness, anaemia, renal and cardiac failure, which in the worst cases can be fatal. Parasites can remain inside the liver even if you get over the fever, and malaria can recurr years later. The most dangerous type is *malaria tropica* (parasite: Plasmodium Falciparum). Except for the highland areas, where you are safe from the bite of the Anopheles mosquito, malaria is endemic in Malawi throughout the year. Tablets are the only prophylaxis which you should start taking two weeks before departure and six weeks after you return home. It is important to take the tablets regularly!

Chloroquine (Resochin) is the standard precaution, in Malawi however, some agents are immune to Chloroquine. **Proguanil (Paludrine)** is recommended as well.

Mefloquin (Lariam) should under no circumstances be used as a prophylaxis! Mefloquin-resistant organisms do not so far exist in Malawi. It would be irresponsible to culture them in this way. A packet with six tablets of Lariam should however be brought along in case of an infection with malaria.

Additionally you should protect yourself from the carriers of the disease. Use mosquito nets if provided by hotels, or bring your own, although buying one inside the country is less expensive. Also take a mosquito repellent with you. Proper clothes (cotton ones) covering arms and legs, also help to decrease the danger of being bitten.

In Britain, for up to date information on malaria prophylaxis, phone the Malaria Reference Laboratories on **071 636 7921**. In other countries consult a doctor or vaccination centre with knowledge of tropical medicine.

Stay Healthy

Staying in tropical regions at a height of between 300 to 3,000 metres strains the system as much as unknown and unfamiliar agents, non-purified water, strange food, irregular meals, heat and sudden cold. The omnipresent dust and flies cause minute scratches to turn into festering wounds which remain open for weeks. Medical care is often below our standards, even transportation to the next hospital may cause insuperable problems. However, on a more optimistic note, there are enough Europeans and Americans in Malawi in the best of health, to them malaria is less worrying than influenza to us.

Cook It, Peel It or Forget It!
If you stick to the rules, the risk to your health is little higher than that of any holiday.

Rule number one is: cook it, peel it or forget it. On principle eat only what is cooked or peeled, then germs won't have a chance to be taken in via food. Liquids must either be boiled - also the milk in your coffee - or come in bottles or cans. Four different types of Carlsberg beer are available on the market - thus you can live 'healthily' and happily in Malawi. **Water filters** are reliable but awkward to handle, expensive and too heavy to carry over long distances. Chemical water-purifying tablets (Chlorine, Mikropur) protect from bacterial intestinal infections, but not from viruses and amoebas. Iodine is more effective. Be aware of icecubes, ice cream, dairy products, salads, etc., leave them out, if you are unsure. Use boiled water for brushing your teeth and - don't laugh - keep your mouth closed under the shower. Daily **hygiene** is a precaution against inflammations and unwelcome fellow travellers: lice, fleas and bed bugs. Lice eggs, if discovered early enough, can be removed individually or with a special shampoo. Dead bugs, killed by the previous hotel guest, speak for themselves. A first-aid refresher course may turn out to be a life-saving idea.

Snakes, a provoking topic, rouse more excitement than necessary. Far more people die from the bite of the Anopheles mosquito than from snake bites. Snakes are shy animals; if you should come across one of them, stand still or retreat slowly. Only a few species are poisonous and the bite of a deadly venomous snake is not necessarily fatal. In case of emergency dress the wound with a bandage and splint to immobilise the limb to prevent the poison from reaching the heart.

Minor Sins with Major Consequences
Looking back, many illnesses could have been avoided. For example, pneumonia which was caused because the patient could not imagine how cold the nights are. Proper clothes protect from both heat and cold. Stay healthy with a hat! After his return from Malawi a traveller told us about having had serious sunstroke because the wind stole his hat while he was on the back of a pickup. The good old handkerchief around his

head would have saved him from unpleasant nausea and vomiting. Neglecting the intake of water and salt are also minor sins with major consequences. Drink plenty of boiled liquids with added salt. 1.5-litre Coke bottles make ideal water bottles that are light and unbreakable.

Some travellers swear by traditional medicine practised in the countries for centuries. But it is a fact that the average Malawian life expectancy is only 45 years. What keeps this figure so low apart from child mortality?

Preparations for the journey should include a visit to a doctor experienced in the tropics, or one of the special centres for travellers.

In Britain a series of Medical advice centres are run by British Airways, in conjunction with MASTA (Medical Advisory Services for Travellers Abroad). In addition to inoculations, the centres sell various health essentials such as malaria pills, insect repellent, and sterile instrument pack. The latter is recommended for travel in Malawi, where you must ensure that sterile needles are used as a precaution against AIDS.

MASTA offer a variety of services, including a Concise Health Brief which gives up to date advice on how to stay healthy in the areas you are visiting. Forms are available from Boots or other chemists, or phone 071 631 4408. MASTA also sells basic tropical supplies and sterile instrument packs. Their address is Keppel ST, London WC1E 7HT.

Vaccination centres in London are:

- British Airways Medical Department, 156, Regent St, London W.1, tel. 071 439 9584. Open 8.30 to 16.00.

- Thomas Cook Vaccination Centre, 45 Berkeley Street, London W.1., tel. 071 499 4000.

- Trailfinders immunisation centre, 42-48 Earls Court Rd. London W8 6EJ. Open 10.00 - 13.00, 13.30 - 16.30, Monday to Friday.

AIDS and Hepatitis B prevention kits (sterile needles, etc.) are available from SAFA, 59 Hill St, Liverpool, L8 5SA, tel. 051 708 0397.

In London the main Centre for Tropical Medicine is:
Hospital for Tropical Diseases,
4 St Pancras Way,
London NW1 (tel. 071 387 4411).

Do not forget to see your dentist before you leave, dental treatment is extremely expensive in Malawi.

Medical Insurance

You should take out additional **travel insurance**, the premiums are surprisingly low. Apart from medical treatment expenses and hospital care, the return journey in case of accident or serious illness will also be covered. Membership to the Red Cross not only supports the aid organization but also guarantees your return journey in the event of illness. Take enough traveller's cheques to cover additional expenses which will be reimbursed if you are properly insured.

Vaccinations

Get your vaccinations three months, or at the latest 6 weeks before departure.

1. Yellow Fever: compulsory only if you come from endemic regions. If you intend travelling to other Central or East African countries, you should be inoculated against it.
2. Cholera: A serious intestinal infection caused by contaminated food and water. Cholera prophylaxis is not obligatory for Malawi, but recommended. The dates of the vaccination against yellow fever and cholera should not be too close together.
3. Typhoid: oral vaccination against bacterial diarrhoea should be taken one week before you start with the malaria prevention, that is to say, 3 weeks before you leave.
4. Polio: check whether your protection against poliomyelitis is still valid.
5. Tetanus: the same applies to the series of injections protecting against lockjaw. The vaccination is valid for one year.
6. Hepatitis: Gamma globulin injections provide a partial protection against infectious hepatitis type A transmitted by the intake of contaminated food. The more dangerous hepatitis type B is transmitted in the same way as AIDS. Vaccination against hepatitis type A is recommended for longer trips.

7. Diphtheria: Vaccination against this highly contagious disease is especially advisable for backpack tourists.

Bilharzia

Bilharzia is caused by the larva stage of a parasite carried by tiny water snails. It is associated with still, warm fresh water. Lake Malawi is free from Bilharzia, but it is present in other waters. Never bathe except from the beaches of Lake Malawi. The worms may be taken into the body with drinking water, but they usually penetrate the skin. Bilharzia is one of the tropical diseases developing symptoms after months of infection (the early symptoms of an itchy rash clear up in a few days). Therefore you should have a medical check-up at an institute for tropical diseases once you are back home if you feel ill or have blood in your urine.

Venereal diseases and AIDS, have been the centre of public interest for a long time, thus the precautions should be known.

Medical Kit

1. Malaria preventives. The most important item.
2. Aspirin: the second most important drug serving both as a pain and fever reliever.
3. Diarrhoea: Take Lomotil, but first wash out the bacteria. For that purpose, and to equal the loss of fluid, drink plenty of liquids and replace lost minerals by adding one part salt to 8 parts sugar to your water.
4. Drug against nausea and stomach disturbances.
5. Wound dressings: plasters and sterile bandages for minor and major wounds.
6. Antiseptic cream.
7. Disposable syringes: for those terrified by AIDS.
8. Vitamin tablets.
9. Suncream or oil: Or make your own with 1/2 litre of olive oil and the juice of one lemon.
10. thermometer: protect it from breakage.
12. Drug against cold-related illnesses.
13. If you are on a prescription at home make sure you have a good supply with you, e.g. anti-histamine drug.
14. An International Vaccination Certificate is obligatory for admittance to the country and is helpful in case of hospital treatment.

Keep in mind that medicines are unobtainable in most places in Malawi. Sometimes you may be asked for drugs from people convinced that European medicine is good medicine. Unless you know what you are doing it is best not to share it. Your medical kit can always be donated to a hospital at the end of your holiday.

In Malawi even the smallest clinic carries the name hospital. Sometimes there is no full-time doctor in charge, but a medical assistant who has dealt with tropical diseases for many years can still be of help to you. Well-equipped hospitals are in Blantyre, Mzuzu, Lilongwe (Likuni Hospital) and Livingstonia. Nyika National Park has a full time medical assistant.

ACCOMMODATION

Hotels

Better hotels offer accommodation of European standard and prices. Some are situated off-shore of Lake Malawi, offering water sports facilities. Luxury hotels with courteous service, swimming pools, air conditioned rooms, restaurants, telephones (which may also be used by the public) are to be found in the major towns of Blantyre, Limbe (near Blantyre), Lilongwe and Zomba. The chain of the **Malawi Hotels** includes seven excellent hotels for which reservations can be made at the Central Reservations Office, PO Box 376, Blantyre, tel. 620071 or 620812.

For a detailed description of the individual hotels see *The Cities*.

Rest Houses and Private Accommodation

Budget travellers may stay at the **Government Rest Houses** or at a few privately run guest houses throughout the country. Service, management and cleanliness are exemplary. A quick examination of the rooms is, however, advisable. Most of the Rest Houses provide also a simple breakfast. If lunches and evening meals are not available, you can prepare your own meals or hand over the ingredients to the 'chef of the house' to prepare them for you, a custom, you will soon get used to. For reservation apply to the District Commissioner of the respective town. Rest Houses are to be found in Chinteche, Chitipa, Dedza, Kasungu, Karonga, Likoma, Mzimba, Mzuzu, Ngabu, Ntcheu, Nkhata Bay, Nkhotakota, Rumphi to name a few.

Where to Stay in National Parks
Game Parks and National Parks provide lodges, apartments and huts. Obtain information from:

Chief Game Warden
PO Box 30131
Lilongwe 3

The quality of accommodation varies considerably. At Chilinda Camp (Nyika National Park) chalets, where a blazing open fire gives off comforting warmth on cold nights, are let for 70 kwacha per day. Lifupa Camp at Kasungu National Park; offers similar comfort, even a swimming pool belongs to the facilities. Mwuu Camp in Liwonde National Park situated at the Shire River offers more basic accommodation.

Campgrounds
Malawi has two public camp sites, one in Zomba and the other in Lilongwe at the a golf course. Some guest houses offer camping in their gardens; the price is not much different from that of double rooms. Any kind of igloo tent is an advantage, since it does not require pegs. Its inner tent should be mosquito-proof. In cheap hotels we simply set up the inner tent inside the room for protection against mosquitoes, bed-bugs and other insects. In the national parks there are campsites for your own tent, or tents may be hired for the night.

MALAWI THROUGH THE PHOTOGRAPHER'S EYE

Great care must be taken in what you choose to photograph. Any bridges, buildings, electrical installations, roads, airports are strictly prohibited. Anything that could be considered sensitive for national security is banned. The authorities strictly enforce the observance of these regulations.

Journalist activities are also illegal, not only taking pictures, but also investigating matters of media interest. As far as taking pictures is concerned, the police are obliging provided the pictures are of tourist interest. Photographs showing Malawi in a positive way, such as market scenes, a fisherman's boat or a beach are more than welcome. Pointing the camera at a scantily dressed person however is not acceptable.

As a rule, never take pictures of a person in uniform. If you are in town, it is best to go up to a policeman for advice. Your film is likely to be finished earlier with official help than without. Similarly, ask permission to take portraits, some people don't like it. Though the picture looses its spontaneity, none is offended. Sometimes people ask for money in return for the favour. It is up to you how you handle this, but please keep in mind that 1 kwacha is the equivalent of a day's wage.

What is there to do when the police take action against an overly bold photographer? We advise you to claim innocence. The worst that may happen is that you will be arrested, questioned and deprived of your films. We know of two such cases in which the culprits were released after 24 hours.

In any case, it is best to avoid conflict with the authorities. It is a question of respecting the country which you came to visit without patronizing.

CULINARY DELIGHTS

Chambo, Samosa and Nsima

Malawian cuisine is very diverse, influenced by different African tribes, Asian and British cooking, with additions from neighbouring Mozambique with its Portuguese background. This mixture is completed by native fruits.

We collected some recipes of traditional Malawian cooking for your interest.

Fish

Lake Malawi provides this main ingredient of the Malawian cooking Further sources are Lake Chilwa, Lake Malombe and several rivers, e.g. the Shire. The possibilities of preparation are manifold. Though many fish have European common names the majority of the species are endemic to Africa. The biggest fish is the Lake Tiger (*Ncheni*). Lake Salmon (*Mpasa*), *Ngumbo*, *Kampango* and *Vundu* are further species which are allowed to be caught.

The Chambo, a kind of perch, is very abundant. Delicious fried or boiled in one piece or cut in fillets and seasoned with garlic or curry.

However, small fish of the size of sardines account for the main share of fish eaten. The fish are sun dried to preserve them so that they can be transported to areas far away from the lake. Trout were introduced into the rivers early in this century and record-sized fish have been caught.

Dried Fish in Chilwa Sauce

2 good-sized dried fish
2 cups of nsima (see below)
2 onions
1 egg
1 large tomato
1 onion
40 g butter
40 g plain flour
juice of one lemon
spices
salt

Cook the fish and tomato until tender. Drain the liquid and bring to the boil. Remove the flesh from the fish and set aside. Beat the egg and mix with nsima, add water, onions (chopped), spices and salt. Add the fish carefully and make a firm dough. Form into balls. Cook the balls in the liquid for 10 minutes. Remove the fish balls.

Melt butter in a pan, add the flour, stirring continously. Add the liquid and bring to a boil, stirring well. Blend with lemon juice. Serve both fish balls and Chilwa Sauce hot.

Avocados

The colourful selection of fruit includes banana, papaya, mango and avocado. Avocados are a major ingredient of Malawian cooking.

Peyala Soup

2 medium or large ripe avocados (*peyalas*)
2 cups of chicken stock
1/2 cup of cream
juice of one lemon
1 tbs curry powder (see below)
salt
crushed chillies

Cut the avocados in half and remove the pit. With a teaspoon remove the flesh from the skins. Mix the flesh with lemon juice to prevent from discolouring, add cream and curry powder. Mash together and season with the crushed chillies. Blend together with the stock and bring to the boil. Serve hot.

Vegetables

Cassava, otherwise known as manioc and originating in South America, makes both a tasty entrée and a snack. The root is peeled (the peel is poisonous), cut in half, lightly boiled then deep fried and seasoned with lemon and chillies. The leaf makes an excellent green vegetable.

Maize is the basic ingredient for *Nsima*, the traditional staple. Stir water into the cornmeal until syrupy. Bring to a boil and add more cornmeal, stirring constantly until the batter is solid and white. Serve hot. Form small balls out of it and eat it together with cabbage or spinach or curries. This recipe sounds simple, but it does not turn out well the first time. Some practice is needed. The batter must lose its yellowish colour, must not be sticky or taste bitter and not be lumpy. Have Nsima in the mornings, instead of porridge with milk and jam.

On Likoma Island the headman of the village next to where we camped gave us plantains to welcome us. For days we had to eat this nutritious but flavourless fruit until we were fed up with it.

Ntochi Casserole
8 bananas (ntochi)
8 slices ham or bacon
1 tbs plain flour
2 cups milk
1 cup grated cheese
juice of one lemon
spices, salt
2 tbs butter
2 egg yolks

Place one tablespoon of the lemon juice in a bowl with the egg yolks. Heat slowly and beat well, until the mixture thickens. Add the butter and the flour, beating constantly. Slowly add the milk, stirring all the time until the sauce is well cooked and smooth. Add salt.

Peel the Ntochi (bananas) and wrap each in a slice of ham. Place into the casserole and pour the sauce over the bananas. Sprinkle the grated cheese on top and bake in the oven for about twenty minutes.

Curry and Samosas

Curry powder clearly reveals the Asian influence on the Malawian cooking. This spice is actually a mixture of spices such as chilli, coriander, black and white pepper, caraway-seeds, mustard seeds, cinnamon, fennel and cloves. Curcuma (turmeric), which is used to substitute saffron, gives curry powder its yellow colour.

Most restaurants offer a varied menu of curries, in their tasty Asian dishes.

Samosas, small triangle shaped pastries have an endless variety of fillings. All fillings have one ingredient in common: curry. The batter for the pastry is made of self-raising flour, salt, oil, lemon juice and water. Shaping the pastry properly, however, requires crafty hands.

PART IV

The Cities

KARONGA

The first kings of Maravi came from the House of Karonga in the north of Malawi. For many travellers from Tanzania Karonga is the first encounter with Lake Malawi after kilometres of dusty roads. There has been a fort and a customs post here from the time of colonization. The streets are either lined with houses with wooden verandahs or with uniformly-built terraced houses.

Karonga is situated in the northern plain of Lake Malawi, surrounded by mountain chains which in the constantly changing light appear either as blueish silhouettes or as rugged giants. The two main sights are close together: the football pitch and the market where fish, bananas, rice and beans are sold - important ingredients of Malawian cuisine. At sunrise half the village meets at the shore to wash, either themselves or the laundry. The dugouts leave to go fishing and the women sweep patterns into the dust in front of their houses. Outside Karonga there is a Government Rest House (costing 14 kwacha) with camping facilities a few metres from the shore of Lake Malawi. For two kwacha extra you may use the kitchen with a kitchen boy who takes care of dish-washing and fire-making.

THE OFFICIAL CAPITAL: LILONGWE

Lilongwe is situated on a plateau at a height ranging from 1,000 and 1,350 metres. Primarily the mild climate and the proximity of the river of the same name made this a pleasant location for a boma, an administrative centre at the turn of the century. Indian businessmen settled here and tobacco fields were cultivated in the surrounding areas. However, not until the end of the sixties did the village Lilongwe become the capital of the Republic of Malawi as government departments were moved from Blantyre and Zomba.

The Cities

The new capital was planned to serve as a counterweight to the extreme economic differences between north and south. President Banda succeeded in convincing the western industrialized nations that a new capital was indispensable for the development of his country. Thus the project was carried out with development aid funds. In particular, South Africa supported the project with 45 million US dollars. Bungalows with nice front gardens and tiny thatched houses were built uniformly in the respective neighbourhoods. Embassy buildings, shops, churches and two industrial centres in the north and south complete the picture. What the visitor misses are leisure facilities and, even more important, a real town centre.

Lilongwe has two town centres. One of them is a super-modern and fairly deserted shopping centre on **Capital Hill** outside the town. Here you find a well-stocked supermarket, a PTC (People's Trading Centre), and several small shops. The other contrasting area is a labyrinth of narrow, dusty roads around the market place, with a dozen simple bars. This is the heart of the **Old Town**. The historic part of town starts at the market place where the bus station is situated and winds along Kamuzu Procession Road, past the so-called pubs and drinking halls. At the other side of the river, a couple of offices and shops are situated where the road turns. The majority of the Indian businessmen, who have lived here for generations, have their shops on Kamuzu Procession Road. Most of their shops have wooden verandahs where at night the watchmen in ragged uniforms seek a little warmth from braziers.

Post Office, Shops and Street Dealers

If you come from Sir Glyn Jones Road and turn left into Kamuzu Procession Road in the direction of Lilongwe Hotel, the shopping street lies to your left: here you find a PTC supermarket, banks, travel agencies, a laundry, a hardware shop, a second hand shop, a boutique and the poste restante service inside the General Post Office. During the day, a number of street dealers offer African crafts in front of the GPO. Amethysts, topaz, aquamarines and even rubies from crisis-stricken Mozambique are offered here. However, it is illegal to export precious stones and customs officers may react to the violation of this regulation.

Restaurants in Lilongwe

Annie's Coffee Shop is a fast food restaurant with a mixed group of patrons. Familiar music (pop), friendly service plus good and

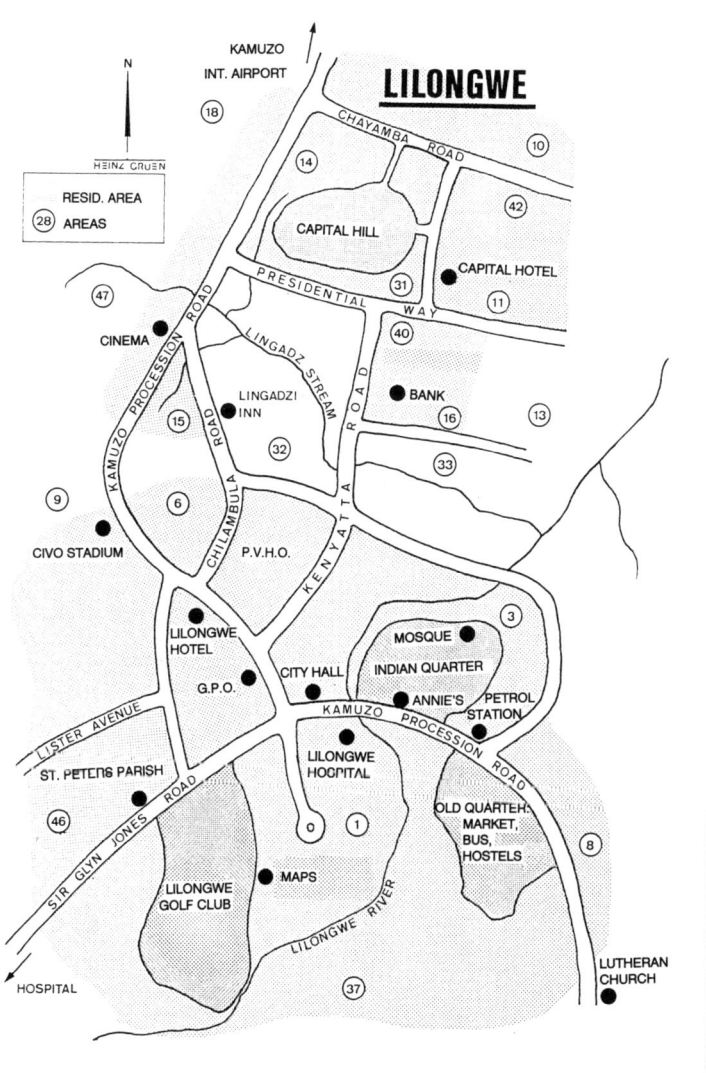

inexpensive food make Annie's the place to go to in Lilongwe. Coffee and tea are really tasty and if the whole of Lilongwe is booked out, you can unroll your sleeping bag in the back room. Try a hamburger with chips and salad (4.75 kwacha) or the chicken curry with rice and salad (6 kwacha). Anyone spending a lot of time at Annie's - which happens often because Lilongwe is where flights and visas applied for are booked - will meet fellow travellers. If you come straight from Europe to Annie's, you might be disappointed by the place, but anybody who has travelled around Africa will adore it.

Further up, near the gasoline station, there are two more restaurants on Kamuzu Procession Road. To your right you will find the Gazebo, to the left the Anamika. The first one serves rice and potato dishes for 7 to 13 kwacha (plus 20% tax/service). On the menu you find omelettes, fish and chips and Malawi's national dish, Chambo, a type of fish. On the opposite side, at the Anamika (next to the petrol station) Chambo costs two kwacha more, but tax and service are included in this price. The Anamika serves various curries and chicken dishes (from 10.50 kwacha upwards), and a Garlic Chicken which is well worth its 20 kwacha. We recommend the Sizzling Portuguese (12.50 kwacha), a dish revealing the proximity to Mozambique, made of beef and vegetables and served with chips or rice.

For lunch you should go to the Golden Peacock (on Lister Avenue). You can relax and eat fairly well in the quiet and shady garden, for example, Nasi Goreng, an Indonesian dish of rice and vegetables (15 kwacha). Further addresses are the Causerie and the Golden Dragon, a Chinese restaurant. The Malingunde inside Lilongwe Hotel is also recommended.

For the hungry budget traveller there are two places to go: the first is the Old Town with its numerous restaurants. Nsima, a maize meal is Malawi's staple food (3 kwacha). The Banja (opposite the off-licence) serves the biggest Samosas in Malawi (0.70 kwacha) and a breakfast (4 kwacha with rice / 3 without) which makes a good lunch, if you order rice with it. Both the selection and the quality of the food are very good, but the service lags behind.

The second possibility to eat an inexpensive snack is the Kainambo Fish and Chips shop (cross the bridge over the Lilongwe river, walk past

The Cities

the post office and turn left into Murray Road). This shop is run by an Indian and is the meeting place for mechanics and lorry drivers. Samosas, fish and chips, plus beef curry are the menu.

Going Out in Lilongwe

The City Hall houses the town's only cinema, if it is not being used for official purposes such as party festivities of the NCP. Films are shown at 20.00 hours on Mondays, Wednesdays and Fridays and at 18.30 hours on Tuesdays, Thursdays, Saturdays and Sundays. The technical quality of the films is acceptable and admission is only 4 kwacha. At regular intervals of four days the films are changed. If you have never been to an African cinema, you should not miss out on this occasion. The spectators clap, laugh and shout during the show.

Classy nightlife as such is almost non-existent; once you know the discotheque inside the Capital Hotel and a handful of restaurants in the large hotels, you have seen it all.

The bars around the market place are flooded by thirsty figures as soon as it is dark. This quarter is loud, dirty and off-putting for most outsiders. The latest meeting place for Lilongwe's young people is the Simba, an overcrowded, simple, but well-kept bar.

The golf club off Sir Glyn Jones Road above the roundabout is more interesting during the day than at night, although there is a bar inside. Expatriate golf fans and also travellers meet here. The caddies are intermediaries between those Indian businessmen and tourists who would like to make a deal.

Hotels in Lilongwe

You will easily find accommodation, unless the government has called its followers to a conference or a celebration. The Capital Hotel (PO Box, 30018, tel. 730444), not to be confused with the nearby Capital Motel, is Malawi's model. It is situated on Chilembwe Road, far away from the Old Town. The hotel provides a restaurant, squash facilities, swimming pool and several shops for the price of 225 to 390 kwacha per night/double room (bookings at the Central Reservations Office, PO Box 376, Blantyre, tel. 620071/620812). The Capital Hotel is part of the chain of Malawi Hotels. Additional facilities at the hotel include a bank where you can change traveller's cheques, even on a Sunday.

The Lilongwe Hotel (PO Box 44, tel. 721866) is centrally located, on Kamuzu Procession Road above the GPO. A single room costs 115 to 160 kwacha, a double room 155 to 200. The whole complex is less luxurious than the Capital Hotel, but offers comfortable accommodation. You can also place international calls from here.

Those who like to socialize in a distinguished atmosphere but cannot afford to pay first-class accommodation, may stay at the camp site at the Golf Club for 10 kwacha per night. You may use the swimming pool, tennis court, bar and, naturally, the golf course. The only disturbance is caused by ants in your tent.

On the opposite side of the main entrance of the Golf Club lies St Peter's Parish. Here one pays 17 kwacha per night for a single room, 22 for a double, 27 for a triple and 32 for a room with four beds (PO Box 294, tel. 720142).

At the Golden Peacock Restaurant and Guesthouse (on Lister Avenue), a middle-range hotel, a double room costs 50 kwacha. Bathrooms are communal.

Inexpensive Accommodation

Inexpensive rest houses are concentrated in the area around the bus station. The best is the City Council Resthouse in front of the bus station, in between the petrol station and the PTC. The showers in the old building are horrible, but the rooms are fairly clean (12 kwacha per night/double room). The recently built brick building is the better choice in all respects (15 kwacha), however, the rooms are often fully booked. You can also try your luck at the market quarter, here the best choice is the Banja (30 kwacha) though the dogs bark throughout the night.

Hospitals

If you are going to get ill do so in Lilongwe, but avoid Kamuzu Hospital and its Health Centre in the Old Town. Take a taxi to Likuni Hospital instead, where you will be treated by two skilled American doctors.

Ongoing Transport

The modern and representative Kamuzu Airport was built in 1983. The road running between Lilongwe and the airport is the best in the country. All international flights land at and depart from Kamuzu

The Cities

Airport. A taxi from town takes half an hour to the airport, the price should be settled in advance with the driver. Air tickets may be booked at several travel agencies in Lilongwe. An extra airport tax in US dollars must be paid.

Car Rental Agencies

Car Hire Ltd	off Chilambula Rd, tel. 723812/723118
SS Rent-a-Car	Kamuzu Procession Road, tel. 721179 or 721213
U-Drive	Lilongwe Hotel, tel. 721866
Hertz	Capital Hotel, tel. 632340/632509

Lorries

Lilongwe is the reloading place for container lorries coming from other countries including Tanzania. At the Kainambo Fish and Chips shop you may be lucky to get a lift from a lorry driver to Dar-es-Salaam or elsewhere. The drivers may be at first reluctant, saying that the extra passengers are not covered by insurance. If so, go and see the manager of Interfreight or AMI. AMI, a forwarding agency, has an office on Kamuzu Procession Road and its head quarters at Kanengo, a suburb of Lilongwe. The man in charge is currently Mr Austin Shaba (tel. 765233 - take bus number 25 via 18 from bus station to Kanengo). Generally though, you arrange the details with the driver, to whom you pay a small sum in US dollars. You should be aware that the drivers rarely stop, always drive at full speed, even on sandy tracks, and that the engines apparently give off a major part of their heat into the front of the vehicle. As it is also extremely warm outside you can imagine how hot it gets inside.

THE UNOFFICIAL CAPITAL: BLANTYRE

On October 25, 1876 a group of Scottish missionaries pitched camp in the southern part of Nyasaland and called this patch of earth Blantyre, after the birth place of the missionary and explorer David Livingstone. However, the official date of the foundation of the town is 1895. Blantyre did not become the capital, but was the largest, most important and most interesting town of the small country.

Blantyre is set in the Shire Highlands, at a height of 1,100 metres, has 350,000 inhabitants, and is closely connected with Limbe, 8 km away.

The Cities

Chileka Airport, situated 18 km outside the town lost its status as an international airport when Kamuzu Airport in Lilongwe was opened. Nevertheless, the visitor who stays long enough in the country, will sooner or later come to Blantyre. Although Blantyre is a reasonably big city, you can orientate yourself in the centre by the triangle formed by Haile Selassie Road, Victoria Avenue and Glyn Jones Road. The city has few obvious tourist attractions, apart from the **Museum of Malawi** and **St Michael's Church**. But anyone who is interested in the first European explorers will find Blantyre a fascinating place.

The government's efforts to shift the country's economic centre from the south to the north did not push Blantyre into second place. The annual **Independence Celebrations** on July 6 are still held in Blantyre's Kamuzu Stadium where 50,000 spectators witness traditional dances, military and school children's parades and listen to speeches. Tickets for the marathon show are available free of charge at Development House, at the corner of Victoria and Henderson Avenue.

A number of tin-roofed houses with verandahs and the town hall, all built at the turn of the century, are situated at the corner of Haile Selassie Road and Victoria Avenue. These buildings previously housed several colonial departments.

The visitor interested in history should visit the above mentioned St Michael's and all Angels Church. The friendly sexton gives the visitor a comprehensive survey of the foundation of the congregation and the construction of this most astonishing church. The redbrick church, a mixture of different styles, was built between 1888 and 1891 by Reverend Scott, who had never before been involved in any building project. You will find this church off Chileka Road, several hundred metres away from the bus station. Coming from the Grace Bandawe Conference Centre, the way into town leads past the church.

A small museum with the promising name National Museum stands remote from the road running from Limbe to Blantyre in Chichiri. It is open from Tuesday to Sunday, from 10.00 to 16.00.

Inexpensive Accommodation

Our answer to simple, but well-kept accommodation in Blantyre is the Grace Bandawe Conference Centre which is also called the Church

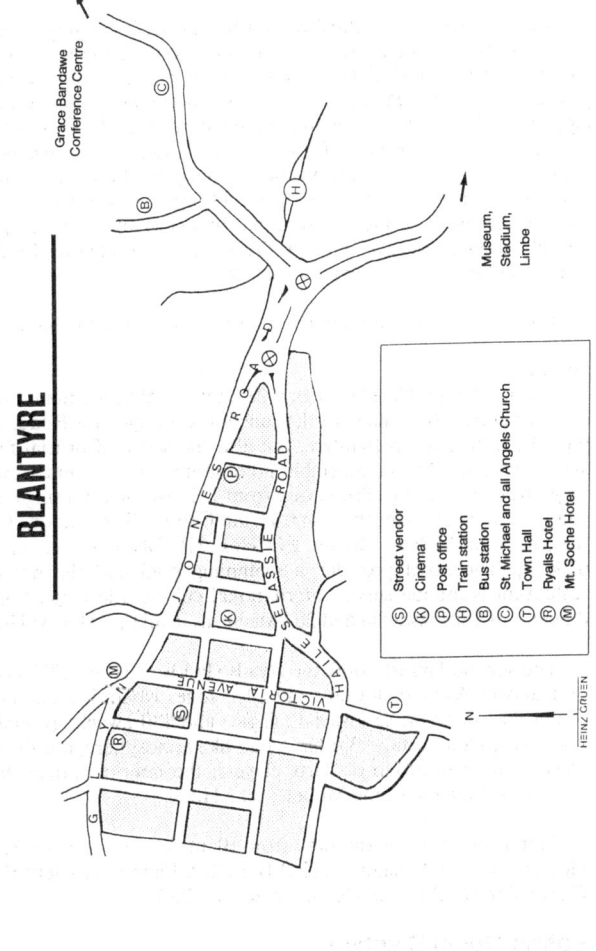

Hostel. It is part of the Presbyterian St Michael's congregation. From the bus station to the hostel is a ten-minute walk along the road to the airport. The beds inside the dormitories are clean, personal lockers are provided and the sanitary facilities are acceptable (10 kwacha per night/bed). A double room with private bathroom and a view of the neat garden costs 40 kwacha. Thanks to the friendly management the atmosphere is very pleasant. In the mornings the breakfast room turns into a meeting place for tourists from all over the world who exchange their experiences during a substantial breakfast of toast and jam and scrambled eggs (3 kwacha). Address: Grace Bandawe Conference Centre, PO Box 413, Blantyre, tel. 634267.

There is also a Government Rest House in front of the bus station.

Hotels

The Mount Soche Hotel (PO Box 284, tel. 635588) is situated centrally on Glyn Jones Road near to the junction with Victoria Road. It is not only the best hotel in Blantyre, but also the scene of official festivities and receptions. The comfortable hotel grants an excellent view of the valley from its gardens. Prices vary from 155 kwacha for a single room to 195 for a double room (bookings at the Central Reservations Office of the chain of Malawi Hotels, PO Box 376 Blantyre, tel. 620071 or 620812). The hotel provides a swimming pool and the hotel-owned restaurant Ndirande serves international cuisine á la carte. Lunch and dinner cost 17.50 kwacha and 20 kwacha, as in all the 'Malawi Hotels'.

The second largest hotel, the Ryalls (PO Box 21 tel. 635955), stands on Hanover Avenue, not far from Glyn Jones Road. It is less luxurious, rooms cost between 85 kwacha (single) and 130 kwacha (double). The hotel bar called Vintage Bar has a pub-like atmosphere, it is the meeting place of a small group of darts players; the interior fittings, however, cannot rival the bar of the Mount Soche Hotel.

Hotels in Limbe, 8 km away from Blantyre, are the Shire Highlands Hotel with a good restaurant (PO Box 5204, Limbe, tel. 640055) and the Chisakalime (PO Box 5249, Limbe, tel. 652266).

Eating Out in Blantyre

In Blantyre you may spoil your palate after a long period in the countryside either in the restaurants of the two major hotels Mount

The Cities

Soche and Ryalls or at the Hong Kong Restaurant or the Melting Pot. The Hong Kong Restaurant (next to Mount Soche Hotel) is more expensive than the first glance at the menu suggests. 10% government tax and 10% service charge are added to the prices. Rice must be ordered extra. Beef curry costs between 5.90 kwacha and 9.30 kwacha, chicken curry 7.50 kwacha. The Melting Pot on Haile Selassie Road is a gourmet restaurant, according to local standards, offering a varied menu. The speciality of the house is prawns.

Local Restaurants

Further down on Haile Selassie Road you will find the Kabula Restaurant, a small café for the local people, which is the counterpart of the Melting Pot. There are lots of these scattered over Blantyre, but we always came back to this one, maybe because the fat Indian proprietor is so friendly. A chicken curry costs 2.50 kwacha, many guests also make do with Nsima, the traditional maize dish. Two more cafés are situated on Livingstone Avenue, Martin's Tasty Food (try the fried rice) and the Tasty Take Away where American burgers are sold for 1.60 kwacha.

Samosas, Indian pastries filled with minced meat or vegetables, are served in all these shops for between 45-60 tambalas. Eat them hot, fresh from the oven. Another inexpensive eating place is the Golden Egg Restaurant where the cooking is also Indian style, with a varied choice of tasty curries, all costing about 10 kwacha. (Glyn Jones Road, near St Davids Street).

Shopping, Post Office, Entertainment

The street dealers have their stalls on Chilembwe Road, between Victoria and Hanover Avenue, a couple of metres away from the Mount Soche Hotel. They sell ebony carvings (please think about the elephants, do not buy ivory!), malachite jewellery and ornate chess boards. Nobody will be offended if you take the time to bargain down prices by 30-40 per cent. On Chilembwe Road there is another PTC supermarket where you can buy all necessary items. The main branch of the National Bank is situated on Henderson Street, at the corner of Victoria Avenue. International calls may be placed from the TeleCom office on Chilembwe Road. Blantyre has two post offices, one lies on Victoria Avenue and the other on Glyn Jones Road. The latter one has a poste restante service where you may collect your mail. Since only a few tourists take advantage of this service there are neither queues nor disorderly heaps of letters. In the vicinity of this post office there is also a gift shop selling African crafts.

The two cinemas are on Livingstone Avenue, films are shown daily at 17.30 and 20.30. From time to time the Apollo shows films produced in Africa. Admission is about 5 kwacha, the seats are comfortable. It is customary that all shows are preceded by the national anthem when you are expected to stand. The Central Bookshop not only provides a large selection of new literature dealing with Malawi, but also has a well-stocked second-hand selection of books about Nyasaland (Malawi before independence). As the books are sold on commission, there is no use bargaining. You may also browse through the books of the reading room of the British Council where European newspapers are available.

Car renting agencies in Blantyre

Car Hire Ltd.	Haile Selassie Rd., tel. 633792 or 635274
SS Rent-a-Car	Glyn Jones Rd., tel. 636836 or 635597
U-Drive Rent-a-Car	tel. 651869 or 651966
Hertz (Blantyre Head Office)	in front of the Mount Soche Hotel
United Touring Co.	P.O. Box 176, tel. 671388
Automotive Products	P.O. 30068, tel. 671855
S. Suleman	Limbe, tel. 650769 or 652830

There is a limited choice of cars, the time of reservation thus becomes a cost factor. Inexpensive cars are booked first; this is particularly true during independence festivities when many foreign guests come to Blantyre.

THE FORMER CAPITAL: ZOMBA

At the turn of the century Zomba was chosen as a settlement by the Blantyre mission of the Church of Scotland because of its favourable climate and its convenient position regarding transport facilities. Soon afterwards it became a boma, an administrative centre and later the seat of the government. The town is characterized by its former function as the capital, which it lost in 1975.

The tin-roofed houses dating back to colonial times compete with one another for the most beautiful verandahs, the greatest porticos and the most extensive glass fronts. State House, built in 1901, was used for official government functions while the Old Residency was the home of the Governor of Nyasaland. The golf club of 1923 is one of the most magnificent buildings of that time and the adjacent golf course is rightly said to be the most beautiful in the country.

Zomba lies at the crossroad between the major highways connecting Blantyre and Lilongwe. The post office and a bookshop are on this fairly tranquil principle road. A turn-off from the main road marks the beginning of the town centre. Here you find the mosque and off the second side street the bus station with the Municipal Rest House opposite. An annexe with double rooms and bathrooms with hot showers was recently constructed next to the bus station. One night costs 15 kwacha. There is also a restaurant.

The business quarter in the town centre is dominated by Indians. The campus of Chancellor College is situated in the east of the town. It is open to the public, granting insight into the possibilities for academic education. Classes are held in the humanities and social sciences, including law. The faculties of science, business and economics are in Blantyre. The bookshop on the campus offers a fairly good selection.

Zomba is growing constantly due to the university and its favourable position on a good road. Its real attraction, however, is its setting among a fascinating landscape.

Zomba Plateau

Zomba is situated at a height of 870 metres on the mountain massif of the same name. Zomba massif is divided into two parts by the **Domasi river**. The northern part is called **Mlosa plateau**, the southern **Zomba mountain**.

Near the main road running from Blantyre to Lilongwe there is a turn-off onto a minor road winding up to the mountain. The way back leads via a different road. After ten minutes of driving you will find a well-kept camp site. The entire plateau is a forest reserve and habitat of a number of species of rare birds and trees.

At the end of the road you come to the Ku Chawe Inn, a modern, luxurious hotel overlooking the plain. It is one of the Malawi Hotels and has to be booked either at Zomba (PO Box 71, Zomba, tel. 2803) or with Soche Tours (PO Box 2225, Blantyre, tel. 635935; prices per night/double room from 130 kwacha upwards). Those interested in trout fishing may apply for a fishing licence at Ku Chawe Inn. The hotel also organizes various tours to the forest reserve.

One of them is a circular tour where leopards might be seen. A hiking trail leads to Mount Zomba, a two-hour walk. The trail winds steeply across the mountain ridge granting spectacular views of the valley one kilometre below. With a clear sky, visibility to the east reaches as far as Lake Chilwa and Mount Mulanje to the south. We climbed the mountain at sunrise and afterwards treated ourselves to breakfast at Ku Chawe Inn (breakfast costs between 10 and 20 kwacha).

FORT JOHNSTON/MANGOCHI

It has been handed down by word of mouth that Maravi, the kingdom of the Caronga, declined after the Arabs and Portuguese discovered the shores of the big lake and used it for the transportation of slaves. In the hey-day of slavery tens of thousands of people were abducted annually from the western shore near to Nkhotakota. Arab dhows were used to ship the slaves across the lake. According to Livingstone, less than a tenth of the slaves survived the march to the Indian Ocean.

The following story illustrates the extent of this exodus. It is said that all mango trees in the area around Nkhata Bay were planted unintentionally. The slave traders fed their captives with mangos whose stones were thrown away.

The people of the Ngoni from the south and the Yao from the east migrated to the depopulated areas. The Yao, traditionally a belligerent tribe, were also involved in the slave trade. Harry Johnston, who originally came as British consul to Mozambique, decided Malawi's fate by turning Nyasaland into a protectorate of the British crown to bring slavery to an end.

Sir Harry was the British gentleman par excellence, despite not having had a conventional education. He started his career in Africa as an artist in Tunis and later always insisted on a clean tablecloth, the best silver and cut glass, even if he were dining in the middle of the bush. He carried out reforms, layed the foundation stone for the administrative machinery which is still in existence, and brought slavery under control. The methods he employed, however, were not gentleman-like; he made a pact with the Arabs and reneged on it later. He deployed his Indian mercenaries for the collecting of taxes and the supervision of forced labour. Though he received little military or financial support, he achieved his aims by 1897. In contrast to Rhodesia there are few reports of violent incidents in Malawi at that time. The social hierarchy he intended to install, namely, that the coutry should be ruled by whites, developed by Indians and worked by blacks, was so successfully made reality that the Chilembwe-Rising of 1915 became an inevitable consequence.

Remains of this era are the ruins of fortified military and police bases. New towns grew around these old forts; the most famous ones are Chiromo, Chitipa (Fort Hill), Liwonde, and Kasungu (Fort Alston). Fort Johnston, the Mangochi of today, is the largest of all.

Mangochi, formerly Fort Johnston

Mangochi is situated on the Shire River between Lake Malawi and Lake Malombe, 130 km north of Zomba and 75 km north of Liwonde. Fort Johnston was built in 1891 to control the river Shire and was moved south to its current location in 1897. Many buildings of this time have been preserved, e.g. the old club house which is today a small museum. The **Queen Victoria Clock Tower** of 1903 became a reminder of the crew of the vessel Vipya which sank during a storm in 1964. The **Lake Malawi museum** shows some ethnologically interesting exhibits and shipping artifacts.

Nkopola and Makopola: Water Sports Facilities

Nkopola Lodge, a beautiful hotel, is situated on the shore of Lake Malawi, 25 km north of Mangochi and 40 km south of Monkey Bay. Prices start at 120 kwacha per night, but the luxury facilities justify such expense. Water sports facilities are excellent: sailing and motor boats, water ski, catamarans and diving equipment are available for renting.

Four kilometres away you find Makokola Club which is in no way inferior. The facilities for water sports meet high expectations, unless you care about environmental pollution caused by the motor boats. Nkopola Leisure Centre also provides a clean and looked-after camp site for 21 kwacha per night.

Booking and information:
- Nkopola Lodge: Soche Tours, PO Box 2225, Blantyre, tel. 635935,
- Makokola Club PO Box 59, tel. 584228.

LIVINGSTONIA

There is no doubt that Livingstonia is worth the journey. The spirit of the missionary pioneers is still alive.

The village is situated at a height of 1,000 m and is accessible from two sides. One possibility is to cross the Nyika Park. From the camp site in the heart of the park near the village of Chilinda travel eastwards until the surfaced road ends. From here only four-wheel-drive vehicles or hikers can procede. Though the distance from the camp site to Livingstonia is 40 km as the crow flies, the constantly ascending and descending trail makes the journey very slow.

The second and better known route is from the lake side. Whether you arrive by express bus from the north or south or by ferry across the lake does not matter since you always end up at Chilumba, where a local bus takes you to Chitumba. Ask the bus driver, he will let you off at a minor turn which is easily missed. Only a tiny sign at the side of the road indicates that it leads to Livingstonia. Next to the turn off there is a simple restaurant where you may set up your tent. Hitchhikers should try to get a lift from the restaurant. There is no bus connection to Livingstonia and hardly any traffic in the afternoon. A lift usually costs between 1 and 2 kwacha.

From behind the restaurant a serpentine road from 1902 with exactly 20 bends winds through the bush to Livingstonia plateau. The track is about 18 km long, but the local people know a shortcut which is half the distance. At the top you will find the Livingstonia Guest House, costing 8 kwacha (10 kwacha for a tent). You can either eat a hot meal at the Guest House or buy biscuits, Coke, crisps and pineapples at the village shop. Sometimes even petrol is available. The Gorden Memorial Hospital is nearby should you need treatment, it was finally built in 1911.

The sights include the Stone House, a museum, which was built for Dr Laws, head of the mission in 1903 (closed at lunch time), a church (whose windows reproduce Livingstone's arrival at Lake Malawi) and the Manchewe falls and caves with African cave-paintings. Except for the falls all the sights are close together. You should not miss the museum in the Stone House where you can easily spend an hour learning about Malawian history. The artifacts may be touched. The way to the waterfalls is difficult to describe. Take a guide and ask him to show you the caves, too. Don't forget to take a torch for the caves and warm clothes as it can get cold in the evening hours.

PART V

National Parks and Natural Wonders

CAPE MACLEAR

Nankumba peninsula rises up from the shores of southern Lake Malawi. Its eastern shore is cut by a bay whose bright boulders rise from the clear water. Since the beginning of the century this natural harbour has been a landing place for boats. The harbour village soon became a *boma*, the seat of the district government. The village Monkey Bay, named after the bay of the same name, is an important place for the tourist. Not only is it the starting-point for a cruise on board the *Ilala* or *Mtendere* but it is near one of the most beautiful places in Malawi: Cape Maclear, Malawi's unique **underwater national park** and the scenes of breathtakingly beautiful sunsets.

Lake Malawi National Park

Cape Maclear national park covers the northern part of Nankumba peninsula and includes twelve small off-shore islands. Occasionally elephants, antelopes, big cats or hippos may be viewed in the park, but its main attractions are the different species of reptiles and birds. Cormorant colonies breed on **Mumbo Island** and otters are sighted at **Otter Point**. The setting of the reserve is perfect. Evergreen mountains rise steeply from the water's edge. Sandy beaches, stony coasts and swamps alternate with each other. However this is surpassed by the beauty underwater.

Green reeds rooted in the fine sand grow below the surface and fish glisten in the colours of the rainbow. A big, deep-blue fish swims through a school of restless, orange-coloured fish and a red fish builds a nest. The intruder with diver's goggles feels that he is in a fish tank. No wonder: 10 per cent of all exotic fish are imported from Malawi.

According to the World Wide Fund for Nature (WWF), Lake Malawi houses over a thousand species of fish. The exact number is still unknown and new species are being discovered. Until today about 400 species of fish from only seven families have been discovered, most of them are endemic. In cooperation with the WWF Malawi founded Lake Malawi National Park to preserve this unique variety of fish. Proceeds from tourism are used to maintain the reserve. The local fishermen must not fish near the coastline. Larger boats shall in the future be provided for lake fishing. Rangers are employed to prevent illegal fishing and pollution, often caused by tourists. The future will show whether this concept will be successful.

Getting There
Buses to Monkey Bay operate from all major towns. The journey from Zomba takes four hours, from Blantyre six. Visitors are collected at Monkey Bay. If you come by car, take the M18 from Mangochi to Cape Maclear. Lake Malawi National Park is 232 km from Lilongwe, 251 km from Blantyre and 168 from Zomba.

The Stevens'
The Stevens run a simple camp which consists of several redbrick buildings and a restaurant on the beach in the park. With their overloaded pick-up they collect tourists at Monkey Bay twice a day. What an adventurous journey; legs and arms, rucksacks and pieces of scrap metal protrude from the pickup! The Stevens brothers cannot cope with the rush of visitors. Everybody who works here carries this 'leave me alone' expression on his face. The newcomers soon scatter in the picturesque fishing village, to the beach or simple huts or paddling in the lake. In the evening they sit at the verandah of the tiny pub waiting for the tasty food. Telephone 0-1301 (Monkey Bay).

Golden Sands
About 3 km away from the camp you can put up your own tent, sleep on the beach or stay in apartments at Golden Sands Camp. Its friendly manager Ado has recently come to the national park to ensure its success. As a biologist and former supervisor of Nyika Park with over 600 employees he is well qualified. Although Ado's task is to improve the camp, the preservation of nature is his great passion.

Golden Sands provides 38 beds and a small bar which is the meeting place for the community. It happens often that a visitor stays longer than he originally intended. The round huts cost 18 to 30 kwacha (single to triple room), the chalets 10 to 20 kwacha. The entrance fee to the park is 1.50 kwacha per person and 4.50 for the car per day. (Tel. 0-1303).

Snorkelling, Swimming and Surfing

Those who have an adventurous spirit should take an oar and paddle to one of the islands. Sitting in a dugout for the first time, you will soon realize how much skill is required to maneuvre them. Leave all valuables on shore on your first attempt. After two days practice you might attempt to fish. We used a 0.4 mm line with one or two medium-size hooks. For bait we took small fish, sold in the village. If you do not catch anything, you may still feed the African fish eagles with the bait. If you do fish, please observe the 100 metre regulation and do not fish off the coastline so that Cape Maclear remains rich in fish.

The days pass much too quickly, they are busy with snorkelling, swimming and windsurfing. Renting a windsurf-board costs 10 kwacha per hour. The wind conditions are suitable for beginners. How much you pay for a dugout depends on your bargaining ability, but 15 kwacha should be acceptable.

Short Tours: Mwalawamphini and Thumbi

A couple of minutes away from the camp a huge boulder called Mwalawamphini speaks of the creative power of nature. It is covered with furrows and lines as if it were created by man.

The hiking trails in the park are strenuous, but the view from one of the mountains rewards you for the effort. A narrow path leads to a remote fishing village and the hippo pool where dozens of hippos may be watched. Watch out for crocodiles, they are never far from hippos! **Thumbi Island**, with many lizards and snakes, is an attractive tour. Never make your way to the island alone as high waves and strong winds can suddenly occur; there are also several underwater currents.

The Monkeys

Monkey Bay has every reason to have been given this name. The tiny monkeys steal anything they can get hold of, after a few days we already disliked these cuddly animals. One of them vanished into a tree after it had stolen our jar of honey. No amount of shouting or shaking of the tree would disturb it. We had hoped that the screw cap would stop the monkey, but the animal opened it without any problems and threw the empty jar at our feet. This was tough because it is difficult to get anything apart from fish and lean chicken in the area.

Food Supply
If you failed to bring enough food supplies with you the village boys will generally oblige. Payment is usually in T-shirts, jeans, shoes or small calculators. Meals can be prepared on the beach or inside the house. Lloyd, the chef of Golden Sands, turns fish and vegetables into true delicacies.

Livingstonia Mission
Cape Maclear was built on the remains of a mission site of the Church of Scotland called Livingstonia. It was established in 1875 and later moved to its current location at Livingstonia. Today one can visit the five graves of the missionaries who died from a disease epidemic and the church, now a heap of rubble. In the chapter *A Mission's Centennial* the history of this mission site is described in detail.

NYIKA NATIONAL PARK

At 6.00 every morning an express bus leaves Karonga in the north of the country for **Rumphi**, travelling south beside Lake Malawi. From Rumphi leads the only road to Nyika National Park.

If you call Chilinda Camp in the park, you might get a lift if one of the rangers is coming to town. If not today, maybe tomorrow. You may however be as lucky as we were and get a lift to the park from town. Our luck was yellow, dreadfully noisy and carried electrical engineering tools. During the 114 km journey on the gravel road we got to know every single bone in our bodies. Renting a car from Rumphi is quite easy and the road is well signposted. Unfortunately there is no public transport between Rumphi and the park. The hostel in Rumphi is not that bad.

Nyika Plateau
Nyika Park is the most spectacular of all the game parks in Malawi. At first sight it seems quite unlike the image we have of African national parks. Rusty coloured rambling chains of hills alternate with forests of fir trees and deciduous trees. Narrow rivers run through the valleys where the ground is swampy. But as soon as the first zebra, antelope or even leopard comes into sight, you may truly feel on safari.

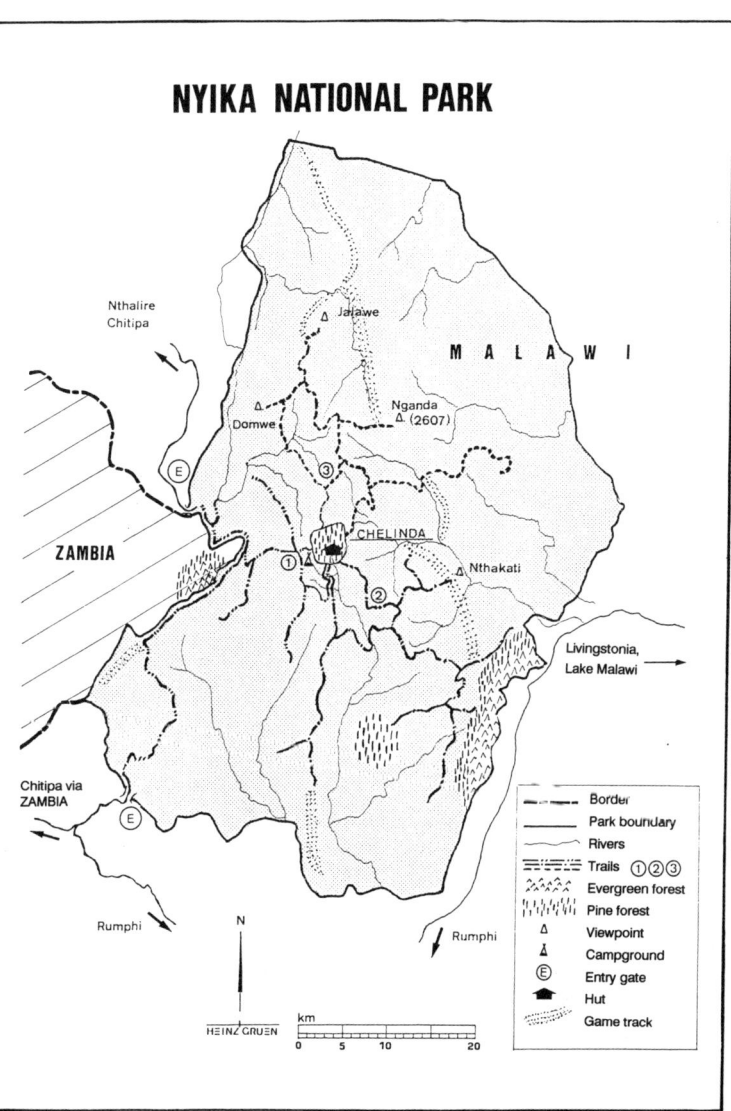

For several thousands of years Nyika Plateau was wooded. Vast areas of forests were destroyed in the last century by fires and deforestation. The timber was needed to smelt iron. Today, controlled steppe fires are set by man to keep the grass short and encourage new growth during the dry season. The remaining protected wooded areas are the home of the blue monkey, the only recorded habitat of the red duiker and 31 different species of birds. If you see a stooping figure peering between the trees, it is likely to be an ornithologist. Nyika Park is the right place for bird-watching. On the plain the main predators are hyenas - you have to be very lucky to see a lion. We are not unhappy about this fact, as the visitor is allowed to explore the hills and valleys on foot.

Three tracks lead to the most beautiful viewpoints. A four-wheel-drive vehicle is not essential, but an advantage. Since it might be dangerous to walk through the national park, which extends over 3,100 (!) km^2, we highly recommend visitors to rent a car. Many animals, e.g. leopards, are best to watch on a night tour.

Chilinda Camp

The main camp is a village of about 3,000 people, mostly rangers and their families who live in wooden huts. Malawi endeavours to preserve nature and has deliberately kept the tourist camp small.

The chalets, apartments for the tourists, are luxuriously fitted and kept tidy. They are solidly built, have two bedrooms and a kitchen. The lounges are comfortable and in the evenings a fire is lit which is very necessary at an altitude of between 2,100 and 2,400 metres where the nights get really cold.

The camp site is set in a forest, 2 kilometres away from Chilinda. All a camper's needs are provided here; sheltered tables and benches, fire places, fire wood, a big water container and clean toilets. In the mornings you can view the game in the valley, if it comes close enough, from the tent at the edge of the forest. Those who want to stay here need a warm sleeping bag. From June to August night frost can occur, but a large open fire and hot tea with whiskey will save you from a cold. The whiskey comes from the shop at the main camp where biscuits and cigarettes are also sold. You must bring all other food you require with you for your stay.

All visitors to the park must report their arrival and departure at the square hut next to the tall pine tree at the little junction. The rangers keep track of all visitors in this way, in case search operations have to be carried out. You can also hire a guide at the reception.

Trout Fishing

One of the rangers accompanied us for the day (6 kwacha). On our way to the river we encountered roan antelopes which fled from us with a loud whistling noise. Without a guide we would have missed the deep, clear river, hidden between green shrubs; even an experienced hiker could get lost here. Fishing is also better with expert advice. We took grasshoppers for bait and soon there was some catch to nibble for the crayfish.

Further Information

The entrance to the national park is 67 km from Rumphi and 135 km from Mzuzu. Visitors must report at the reception at the entrance. The road to the park is not tarred, thus four-wheel-drive vehicles are advisable during the rainy season. Chilinda Camp is 55 km away from the entrance. Fuel supply must be sufficient for the whole journey including tours in the park. Also food has to be brought with you.

Bookings from the Chief Game Warden, PO Box 30131, Lilongwe, tel. 731322.

By the way, a trained biologist works in Chilinda Camp. You are welcome to ask him about the fauna and flora, an opportunity nobody should miss.

KASUNGU, LENGWE AND LIWONDE NATIONAL PARKS

Malawi has five national and game parks whose main purpose is to preserve the rich fauna and flora. We have already described Nyika Park and the unique underwater national park near Cape Maclear. The security rules described below apply to Kasungu, Lengwe and Liwonde National Park.

When you arrive you must report at the entrance of the respective park. Arrival and departure should take place during day light. Walking is only allowed in designated areas or with a guide. Experienced guides,

National Parks and Natural Wonders

familiar with the locality and the game may be hired for one day or a couple of hours for 2 kwacha.

Camping, making fires and picnicking are only allowed in clearly marked areas. Fuel and food supplies have to be brought with you; if you run out of provisions, you might get into serious trouble. The speed limit in the parks is 40 km/h, but to make sure you do not miss anything you should drive even more slowly than this. Besides the expenses for accommodation the visitor has to pay an entrance fee to the parks which depends on the duration of the stay (cars cost extra). Whoever plans to stay overnight should book in advance.

Do not forget that you are among wild animals whose behaviour is unpredictable. A green meadow may turn out to be a swampy hole full of crocodiles, a newborn baby animal is bound to have a protecting mother with sharp teeth and claws or pointed horns.

Kasungu

The Kasungu National Park is situated to the west of central Malawi, on the border with Zambia. It covers an area of only 2,000 km^2, but rivals Nyika for variety of game. The parks are four hours away from each other by car. While its location on the plateau makes Nyika Park so fascinating, Kasungu's vegetation is entirely different.

Lush, green forests, the so-called *miombo*, cover the rolling hills in the north of the park, while the valleys and extensive plains are interspersed with a network of grassy river channels known as *dambos*.

Herds of buffalo whose brown backs rise above the grass, zebra and many species of antelope, such as kudu, roan and sable antelope, graze in the dambos. Impalas are recognizable by their general brownish colour and white underparts. If you are lucky, you might even see an occasional rhinoceros. As they are extremely short-sighted it is possible to stalk them against the wind - not advisable for a *nsungu* to attempt. Big cats, such as cheetahs and leopards, repeatedly cause excitement among the herds. If you cannot see one of these animals yourself, it does not mean that they can not see you.

The park also has large herds of elephant which may be nervous and aggressive, especially if poachers recently hunted them. Elephants are

Cross over by boat to Likoma Island

Paddler in a canoe

120 *"Nzungu! Nzungu!"*: We are the attrac

Children are taken everywhere

Independence Celebration in the Kamuzu Stadium, Blantyre

Life in the country

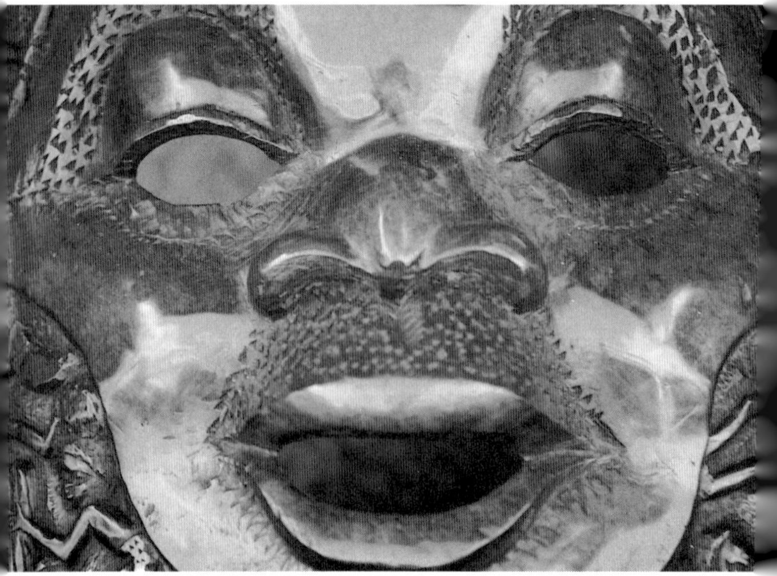

Early morning water gathering at Lake Malawi

National Parks and Natural Wonders

hostile towards man if they feel threatened. The rangers use their loaded guns not only to protect themselves against animals, but also to deal with poachers.

Safaris from Lifupa Camp

It is understandable that hiking tours must be accompanied by an experienced ranger. The 10 km hiking trail in the west of the park is the only exception to this rule. On a safari by car you must under no circumstances leave the car. During the heat of the day all creatures hide from the sun so the best time for game viewing is the early morning or the late afternoon. It is also the best time to take photographs, since light conditions are then most favourable. Guides direct the visitor to the historical sights of the park, such as the remains of an iron smelting kiln, rock paintings (on the Solenje hill) and caves. Night tours are also organized from the camp and a special mini-bus for viewing game may be rented.

Lifupa Camp is situated in the centre of Kasungu Park, 55 km away from the town of Kasungu. The camp overlooks a small lake, and is well-equipped; there is a restaurant, bar, small shop and a swimming pool. Accommodation includes round huts with two or three beds and a bathroom each or camping facilities. Tents can be hired at the camp.

Further Information

Kasungu, 120 km away from Lilongwe, is accessible via the M1. From town to the entrance of Kasungu National Park is another 38 km. Although Lifupa Camp provides a restaurant and shopping facilities, you should bring food supplies with you. The park has no surfaced roads, thus a visit from the middle of January until June is not advisable unless you have a four-wheel-drive vehicle. Do not forget to refuel.

Bookings for Lifupa Camp at Malawi Hotels, PO Box 376, Blantyre, tel. 620071. Obtain information about the national park from Chief Game Warden, PO Box 30131, Lilongwe. There is also a tiny airstrip for private aircrafts near the camp. Seek landing permission from National Headquarters, PO Box 30131, Lilongwe 3, tel. 730853.

Lengwe

It is an hour's drive by car from Blantyre to Lengwe National Park, thus the park is highly suitable for a day tour. It is situated 800 metres lower than Blantyre, its climate is much hotter than that of the town, the average temperature is 35° C. Lengwe National Park is only 130 km² in extent. Due to its small size the animals are used to people and slowly passing cars, which makes the park the ideal viewing-ground for big game.

The major attraction of the park is the relatively rare nyala antelope. There are other species of antelope, baboons and the rare blue monkeys to be seen also. Leopards and hyenas may be viewed at night. If lions and other notable animals have been spotted recently, this is announced at the information board at the entrance to the park. During the dry season the only water available is from four artificial water holes. The game can be viewed at very close range from shaded hideouts.

Four chalets are provided near the entrance comprising of two double rooms and a refrigerator each. The bathrooms are shared. The food supply must be brought in, but there is no cook to prepare meals. Camping facilities are also available.

Further Information

The M8 runs through spectacular landscape from Blantyre to Chikwawa at the bottom of the Shire Valley. From Chikwawa the M8 leads to Lengwe Park. The last 9 km between the main road and the park gate are still un-surfaced.

On its way from Lake Malawi to the Shire Valley the Shire River forms several water falls. One of them is the **Kapichira Falls**, 23 km from Chikwawa and accessible by car. It is the ideal place for fishing. If you have time you should include this side-trip into your tour. Provisions and fuel may be bought in Nchalo, 10 km away from the camp.

Bookings
- Booking Officer, PO Box 30131, Lilongwe 3.
- United Touring Company, PO Box 30193, Chichiri, tel. 634972 offers guided day tours to Lengwe National Park.

Liwonde National Park

Liwonde National Park is rich in animals such as hippo, crocodile and elephant. The park's network of non-surfaced roads is passable from April to November.

Mvuu Camp, a good one hour's drive away from the park entrance, consists of a small bar and a handful of round houses in a bad state of repair. The charming location, however, makes you forget the lack of luxury. Camping is also possible, there are fire places and fire wood in abundance. Food supplies must be brought with you. The park is situated at the lower end of Lake Malombe, about 65 km away from Blantyre. Take the turn-off from the M1 to Liwonde village. As the route is badly sign-posted from there, it is best to ask for directions at the village. From the turn-off it is about 6 km to the park. You can also approach the camp by boat along the Shire River.

GAME RESERVES

Apart from the national parks, there are also a number of game and forest reserves which do not provide facilities for the tourist, a tour to these regions must therefore be planned carefully. Ideally, you should take a guide. One of these areas is the Vwaza Marsh Game Reserve, 55 km west of Rumphi. It is a vast swamp area where elephants, buffaloes, crocodiles and hippos are to be viewed.Nkhotakota Game Reserve furthermore houses different species of big cat. Nkhotakota is accessible from Lilongwe on the M10, but the Ilala and Mtendere also stop here.

Majete Game Reserve offers a single apartment for tourists. It is about 45 km from Blantyre. The Kapichira Falls are in this reserve (see also *Kasungu, Lengwe and Liwonde*). Fishing in the Shire is possible without a licence, the trout season is from May to September. Mwabvi Game Reserve is situated in the southernmost corner of Malawi, 17 km away from Chiromo. Rhinoceroses may be seen here.

Responsible for all national parks and game reserves is the Chief Game Warden, Department of National Parks and Wildlife, PO Box 30131, Capital City, Lilongwe 3, tel. 731322.

HIKING IN THE MULANJE MOUNTAINS

Mount Mulanje rises steeply 3,250 metres southeast of the Shire Highlands. A number of rivers have scarred the mountain ridge. The Chambe and the Mchese flank the mountain. To the south of the **Mulanje foothills** tea is cultivated. The Mulanje cedar, a source of high quality wood, is slowly becoming extinct.

Approach
From Blantyre it's best to take the road via Thyolo. About 10 km north of Mulanje village (hospital, golf course, post office) a branch of the M1 leads past tea plantations, through the valley of the Likhubula river to the Likhubula Forest Station, where all mountain hikers have to report. The station is situated at a height of 890 metres, from here you can climb up to nearly 3,000 metres. For security reasons it is not advisable to leave a car at the beginning of the hiking trails at Tuchila or Malosa.

Preparations
At the Forest Station porters can be hired to carry backpacks and food. Those who are not familiar with that kind of service may flinch at employing the young men. Yet with some of the hiking trails being steep and tourism being a good source of income, you should feel free to accept their services. Tariffs are fixed to ensure adequate payment for their work, however not according to our standards. 3 kwacha uphill, 2 kwacha downhill per day. Hikers must provide the porters with food.

Clothes and sleeping bag should be warm as it can get really cold at these higher altitudes. With regards to planning the hiking route it is inadvisable to ask the porters for advice. For understandable reasons they want to reach the next camp as fast as possible instead of leading you along scenic but perhaps arduous paths. Returning hikers are a better source of advice.

The huts have to be booked in advance at the Forest Station. In this way the Forest Department, which is responsible for rescue operations, can keep track of the hikers. Camping is possible, but open fires are not allowed because of the danger of forest fires. However, the opportunity to catch some camp atmosphere next to fireplace make the mountain huts, which are in perfect condition, pleasant places for rest and relaxation.

The Hiking Trails
The first stop is usually made at Chambe Mountain Hut (1,900 metres above sea level, a four-hour tour). On this day tour you pass the waterfall of the Chapaluka river where two small basins invite you for a swim. The path is so steep that those who are not fit will be exhausted after four hours of hiking. To the next rest house, Tuchila Hut, it is a five-and-a-half hour walk (2,000 metres above sea level).

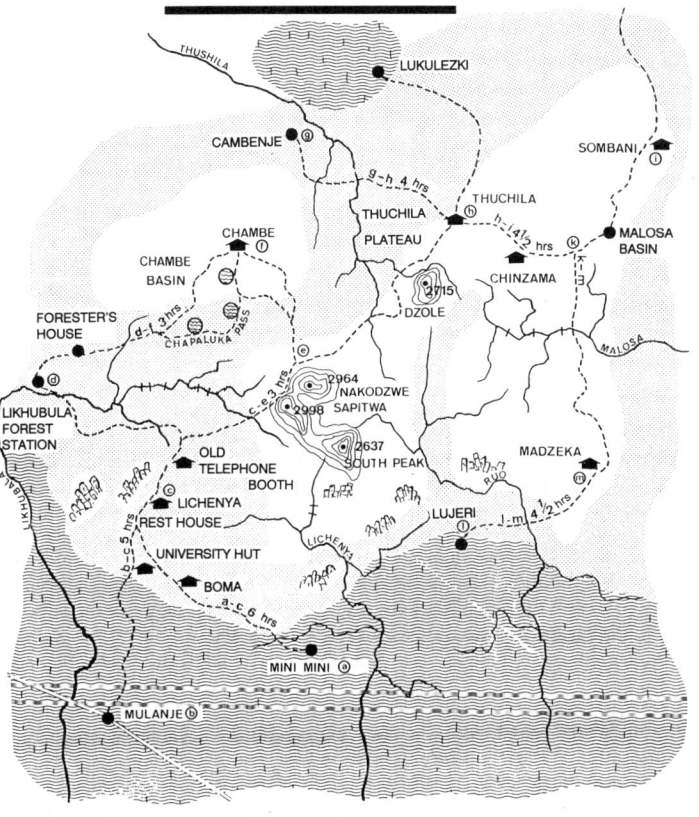

From there you may continue your tour either to the Sombani Hut (five-and-a-half hour walk) or to the Madzeka Hut (four-and-a-half hours away) still at a height of between 1,700 and 2,000 metres. The way back leads either via Lichenya Rest House in the southwest directly to Mulanje or via the steep Lichenya Path ending at Likhubula Forestry.

Ask for a trail map at the Department of Surveys, PO Box 349, Blantyre. Further information is available from The Mountain Club, PO Box 240, Blantyre.

LIKOMA ISLAND

Likoma Island is situated a couple of kilometres off the coast of Mozambique. Although surrounded by Mozambican waters the island is part of Malawi. It can only be reached by boat (though there is a tiny airport).

Sailings to the island are on Wednesdays and Sundays on the Mtendere and Tuesdays and Saturdays on the Ilala. As there is no harbour the boats anchor offshore. From all directions dugouts paddle towards the vessel to take sacks of goods on land or to sell fish. With a loud, buzzing sound both longboats (originally there were four of them) are lowered to the water. In less than half an hour of bustling activity new passengers have boarded the boat and those heading for the island have left. Boarding one of these boats with rucksack and camera is quite an acrobatic exercise. We were glad to set foot on firm ground again. A dozen backpacks are thrown ashore, on to the tiny paradise island, which is a mere heap of sand and stones, dominated by ancient baobab trees.

It is said that Likoma at one time used to be a centre of witchcraft and sorcery until the **Likoma mission** was established putting an end to superstition in 1885. At the beginning of the century a brick church, rivalling Westminster Abbey in its overall size, was built to counterbalance natural religions, an unbelievable undertaking. In Neo-Gothic style the church peeks out from between two hills, over-sized and out of place. The carvings come from the Bavarian Alps, the bricks from Canterbury, the soil from Jerusalem and the wooden cross from Zambia, from a tree which had allegedly grown above Livingstone's heart. The silvery metal sheet roof glistens on the lake's surface.

From the belfry the island's natural harbour can be viewed. If the door is locked the sexton has taken the keys, for the bats must remain undisturbed during the heat of the day. He also keeps the key for the dark wooden walled library, an extension of the cloister.

Jofuh Bay

Jofuh Bay is a dusty two-mile walk from the landing beach, past the secondary school. It is the best place to camp for a couple of days. The warning that the bay is target for robberies may only have been a rumour spread by inhabitants from the other bays who are competing for visitors. The view of the white granite boulders scattered in the crystal-clear water and the sandy beach at sunset, all melting into a rich play of colours, makes up for the long walk. The most important daily happenings are the sunrise above the lake and the sunset above the mountains of the island.

Swimming and Snorkelling

Fortunately there is always someone who speaks English and is willing to interpret. The village people are noticeably friendly, especially the children; you will get used to them watching your every move. Fishermen in their dugouts stand out against the horizon. Birds revel in the last sunbeams of the setting sun. During our few days' visit we got into the routine of village and camp life, making fire, preparing meals, washing the dishes with sand and water, boiling drinking water (never to be forgotten!), chatting, swimming, snorkelling (bring goggles), buying wood and food from the villagers.

Our camp consisted of a couple of sleeping bags arranged near the fire (tents are unnecessary in the dry season), some aluminium dishes and a lot of sand. If travelling on your own, you are very likely to meet up with others on board the boat. Making friends and finding a companion is easy. With regards to robbery, beware of crows which steal everything they can get hold of, even if it is of no use to them. After darkness place your belongings as near to the fire as possible. A nylon string fixed to the backpack and tied around your foot is an acceptable substitute for a guard.

The characteristic Malawian friendliness revealed itself to us when someone offered to gut the chicken he had just sold us. We could easily live very cheaply in this remote part of the world, eating the island's products such as rice, eggs, bananas and fish. Yet we were glad of the food we had brought with us. With self-raising flour we experimented making our own banana bread. Spices, sauces, vegetables and powder soups added some colour to our menus.

Walking around the island takes only a few hours. If you do not mind snakes (always carry a long stick), you can climb to the highest point within an hour. From the top you have a fascinating panoramic view. The east side of the island is relatively untouched, the northern part is already explored and, looking to the west, you will see Likoma's biggest village.

Where to Stay

In the main village you will find several rest houses which are small, but fairly clean. Before booking a room check on electricity and water supply. The Akuzike (situated in the market place, a seven-minute walk from the landing place) offers simple accommodation for 6 kwacha. Next door is the island's only refrigerator, that is to say, the only place to drink a cool beer. Fire wood is as rare as refrigerators, sometimes Mozambicans ship over wood in tiny boats. There are a number of Mozambican refugees who, from a safe distance watch the situation in their home country. Poverty is what they all have in common. Thus spare clothes, equipment or food is very valuable to the people in exchange for food or services.

GLOSSARY

English	Chichewa

The Most Important Word:
thank you — zikomo

Polite Phrases and Words:
hello — moni
how are you — uli bwanji
I'm well — diri bwino
good-bye — itani bwino
father / mother — ambo / mai
what's your name — zina wanu

To Express a Desire:
please — honde
I'd like — assani ini
I want — difuna
I'm thirsty — dili ndi ludzu
I'm hungry — dili ndi njala
toilet — himbuzi

Questions:
how much... — tengo bwanji...
is it far — odi ndi patali
is it near — odi ndi pafupi
where is... — li kuti...

Answers:
yes — nde
no — ai, iyakayi
good — wino
fine, ok — habwino
very good — li bwino
I come from — dichokera ku

Food:
food — udya

maize porridge	sima
maizemeal	fa
water	adzi
milk	kaka
bread	kata
meat	yama
pork	yama ya nkhumba
beef	yama ya ng'ombe
lamb	yama ya mwana wa hosa
mutton	yama ya nkhosa
rabbit	yama ya kalulu
duck	yama ya bakha
chicken	yama ya nkhuku
rooster	wacha
eggs	azira

Fruit and Vegetables:

fruit	ipatso
avocado	eyala
aubergine	iringanya
banana	zama
beans	yemba
cassava	bwani
chillis	sabola
cucumber	hinkhaka
garlic	dyo
grapefruit	yumwa
lemon	dimu
mushroom	owa
onion	nyezi
orange	alanje
pawpaw	apaya
peanuts	tedza
pineapple	hinanzi
potato	batata, irisi
potato, sweet	batata
pumpkin	zungu
tomato	hwetekere

INDEX

Blantyre	10, 13, 87, 93
Cape Maclear	8, 105
Chilumba	12
Chitumba	102
Dar-es-Salaam	30, 93
Domasi river	99
Fort Johnston	25, 101
Golden Sands	106
Jofuh Bay	135
Kamuzu stadium	32
Kapichira Falls	130, 131
Karonga	61, 87
Kasungu National Park	81, 112
Lake Malawi	7, 19, 51
Lake Malawi Museum	101
Lake Malawi National Park	105
Lifupa Camp	81, 129
Likhubula Forest Station	132
Likoma Island	21, 84, 134
Lilongwe	16, 87
Lilongwe River	90
Limbe	32, 93
Livingstonia	13, 102
Liwonde National Park	81, 111
Majete Game Reserve	131
Makokola Club	101
Manchewe falls	103
Mangochi	101
Monkey Bay	64, 105
Mount Mulanje	100, 131
Mozambique	12
Mumbo Island	105
Murchinson rapids	8
Museum of Malawi	94
Mvuu Camp	131
Mwabvi Game Reserve	131
Mwalawamphini	107
Nankumba peninsula	105
Nkhotakota Game Reserve	131
Nkopola Lodge	101
Nyika National Park	51, 108
Otter Point	105
Rumphi	108
Shire River	19, 130
Solenje hill	129
St Michael's and all Angels Church	94
Stevens	106
Stone House	13, 102
Tanzania	12, 30
Thumbi Island	107
Underwater National Park	105, 111
Vwaza Marsh Game Reserve	131
Zomba	23, 98
Zomba plateau	10, 99

Notes

This travel guide gives helpful information for a different kind of holiday. Stay in rural villages amongst the people; experience the traditional festivals, tea ceremonies, unforgettable jungle taxi trips, the busy markets of Dakar and the Niokolo-Koba National Park. Travel routes and important sights are described as well as essential travel tips.

Bradt Publications
41 Nortoft Rd,
Chalfont St Peter,
Bucks
SL9 0LA
UK.

Hunter Publishing, Inc.
300 Raritan Center Parkway
NJ 08818
USA

ISBN 0 946983 54 2

ISBN 1 55650 308 3

AFRICA HANDBOOK

The Ivory Coast has one of the most charming landscapes and is one of the most culturally interesting countries in West Africa. Wonderful untouched palm beaches, wide tracts of savanna grassland, unique crafts and a belief in progress and deep-rooted tradition are characteristic of the Côte d'Ivoire.

This handbook guides the visitor through this very foreign land, giving suggestions for day trips and tips on how to make a holiday here an unforgettable experience.

Bradt Publications
41 Nortoft Rd,
Chalfont St Peter,
Bucks
SL9 0LA
UK.

Hunter Publishing, Inc.
300 Raritan Center Parkway
NJ 08818
USA

ISBN 0 946983 53 4

ISBN 1 55650 279 6

AFRICA HANDBOOK

Christa Mang introduces a country unspoiled by tourism. Unique is the word that comes to mind when characterizing Zaire's natural wonders. Who wouldn't get a shiver down their spine when faced by an awe-inspiring yet gentle gorilla in the wild?

Bradt Publications
41 Nortoft Rd,
Chalfont St Peter,
Bucks
SL9 0LA
UK.

Hunter Publishing, Inc.
300 Raritan Center Parkway
NJ 08818
USA

ISBN 0 946983 51 8

ISBN 1 55650 273 7

AFRICA HANDBOOK

OTHER AFRICA GUIDES FROM BRADT PUBLICATIONS

Backpacker's Africa - West and Central
David Else
192 pages. Maps, drawings and photos.
ISBN 0 946983 19 4   £7.95

Backpacker's Africa - East and Southern
Hilary Bradt
208 pages. Maps and drawings.
ISBN 0 946983 20 8   £7.95

Through Africa - A guide for travellers on wheels
Bob Swain & Paula Snyder
Approx 300 pages. Maps, b&w and colour photos.
ISBN 0 946983 65 8   £13.95

Guide to Namibia & Botswana
Simon Atkins & Chris McIntyre
Approx 272 pages. Maps and colour photos.
ISBN 0 946983 64 X   £9.95

Camping Guide to Kenya
David Else
208 pages. Maps, drawings and photos.
ISBN 0 946983 31 3   £7.95

No Frills Guide to Sudan
David Else
64 pages. Maps & drawings.
ISBN 0 946983 15 1   £4.95

No Frills Guide to Zimbabwe & Botswana
David Else
70 pages. Maps and drawings.
ISBN 0 946983 16 X   £5.95